ACT 84.10

TAN

TOMATOES

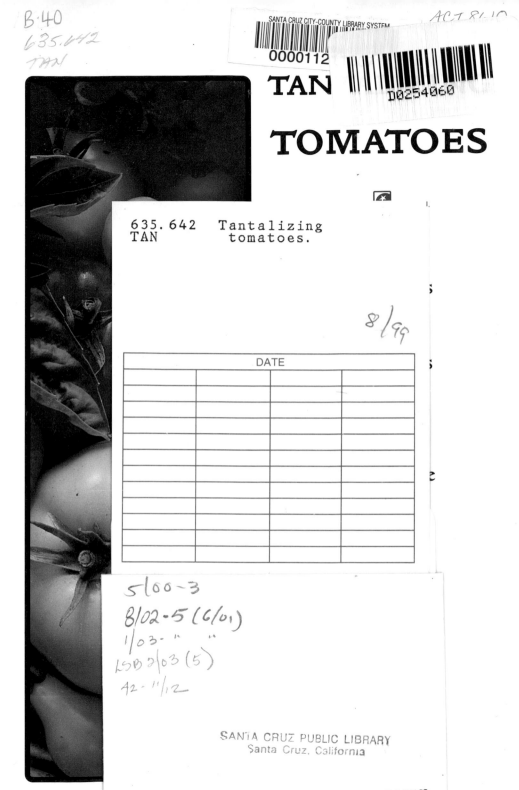

DATE			

FOR THE
ADVANCE
MENT OF
BOTANY
AND THE
SERVICE OF
THE CITY

BROOKLYN
BOTANIC
GARDEN
PUBLICATIONS
· MCMXCVII ·

⟨★⟩ TANTALIZING ⟨★⟩
TOMATOES

Smart Tips
&
Tasty Picks
for
Gardeners
Everywhere

⟨★⟩

Karan Davis Cutler ⁃ Guest Editor

Handbook #150
Copyright © Spring 1997 by the Brooklyn Botanic Garden, Inc.
Handbooks in the 21st-Century Gardening Series, formerly Plants & Gardens,
are published quarterly at 1000 Washington Ave., Brooklyn, NY 11225.
Subscription included in Brooklyn Botanic Garden subscriber membership dues ($35.00 per year).
ISSN # 0362-5850 ISBN # 1-889538-00-0
Printed by Science Press, a division of the Mack Printing Group

Table of Contents

FROM WOLF PEACH TO OUTER SPACE:

Tomato History & Lore

BY KARAN DAVIS CUTLER

OU SAY tuh-MAY-toe, I say tuh-MAH-toe. Or, depending on *where* I live, I might say tomaat or tomate or even pomodoro. And depending on *when* I lived, I might say love apple, Moor's apple or stinking golden apple. Or even amorous apple, which the 16th-century Dutch botanist Dodoens observed, "be of two sortes, one red and the other yellowe, but in all other poyntes they be lyke."

Or I might have called the tomato a wolf peach, from its genus name *Lycopersicon*, a reflection of a long-held belief that the tomato—a member of the nightshade family—was poisonous. That view was largely the result of Renaissance botanists, who, relying on Greek and Roman texts, misidentified and misclassified the tomato. Their errors were copied by popular 16th-century English herbalists, such as John Gerard, who saw no contradiction in writing that while Spaniards and Italians ate tomatoes, the plant was nevertheless "of ranke and stinking savour."

In fact, people were eating tomatoes without fatal consequences well before the fruit made its way to Europe early in the 1500s. Native to the coastal highlands of western South America, the tomato emigrated to Central America and then to Mexico. The Aztecs, according to a contemporary account, mixed tomatoes with chilies and ground squash seeds, a combination that sounds suspiciously like the world's first recipe for salsa.

Tomatoes, native to South America, made their way to Europe in the early 1500s. By the end of the Civil War, they were fairly common fare in American gardens.

'Yellow Pear', right, popular with discriminating 20th-century gardeners, was listed in an 1865 publication on field and garden vegetables of America. Opposite page: paste tomatoes and other ingredients for pasta sauce. The first cookbook to contain tomato recipes was published in Naples in 1692.

Spanish conquistadors carried seeds across the Atlantic, where tomatoes soon flourished in Mediterranean gardens and kitchens. Southern Europeans didn't waste any time taking culinary advantage of the tomato—the first cookbook to contain tomato recipes was published in Naples in 1692—but suspicion of tomatoes persisted into the 19th century in both England and the United States.

The tomato's reputation was partially rescued among English-speaking peoples in the 1750s, when *esculentum*, which means edible, was designated its species name. About the same time, tomato recipes began to appear in British cookbooks, the first in a revised 1758 edition of Hannah Glasse's popular *The Art of Cookery* (though the revisor may have been hedging her/his bets, for the entry is titled "To Dress Haddock after the Spanish Way").

The early American colonists, English to the core, not only brought tomatoes back to this continent but also imported all the popular prejudices about them. While a few adventuresome gardeners grew tomatoes—Thomas Jefferson, who first mentions planting them in 1809, is the most prominent—they were not widely cultivated until after 1830. Suspicion gave way, however, and tomatoes were included in American cookbooks, such as *The Cook's Own Book* (1832), and in garden books, such as the *Shaker Gardener's Manual* (1843) and *The Gardener's Text-Book* (1851).

Alas, the well-known tale of Robert Gibbon Johnson wolfing down a bushel of tomatoes on the Salem, New Jersey, courthouse steps in 1820—a manly effort to prove they were edible—has no basis in fact, according to Andrew Smith in *The Tomato in America* (1994). Too bad, for it's a wonderful story—so good that CBS dramatized it in 1949 in the "You Are There" series—creating the peculiar situation of our being there while Johnson wasn't.

The Landreth Seed Company, which once extended George Washington 30

days on his unpaid bill, is usually credited as being the first company to sell toma-to seeds. *One* of the first is more accurate, but it is true that Landreth's, estab-lished in 1784, was first among present-day seed houses to sell tomato seeds. By the end of the Civil War, tomatoes were fairly common fare in American gardens, and the first Fanny Farmer cookbook, which appeared in the late 1890s, included recipes for tomato soups, salads and sauces without cautions or reservations.

Improving tomatoes was just a step behind eating and selling them. Farm maga-zines urged readers to keep a sharp eye out for the best fruits and to save their seeds. 'Trophy', a large, smooth round tomato, was one of the best early selections; its seeds, which are still available today through Seed Savers Exchange (SSE), sold for a remarkable 25¢ each. Horticulturist Fearing Burr listed two dozen tomatoes in *Field and Garden Vegetables of America* (1865), including 'Yellow Pear', a variety popular with discriminating 20th-century gardeners. The tomato was "universally relished," Burr wrote, but "to a majority of tastes, the tomato's flavor is not at first particularly agreeable; but by those accustomed to its use, it is esteemed one of the best, as it is also reputed to be one of the most healthful, of all garden vegetables."

If the controversy over the tomato being toxic or benign weren't enough, an additional debate has centered over whether the tomato is a vegetable or a fruit. In 1887, the question went all the way to the U.S. Supreme Court in *Nix v. Hed-den*. The real issue was money and protection for American growers: if tomatoes were vegetables, they could be taxed when imported under the Tariff Act of 1883. The Court's botanical knowledge was sound—tomatoes are specialized reproductive structures that contain seeds, in other words, fruits—but it chose utility over botanical technicalities and ruled on the side of American farmers:

> Botanically speaking tomatoes are the fruit of a vine,
> just as are cucumbers, squashes, beans and peas. But

> in the common language of the people...all these are
> vegetables, which are grown in kitchen gardens, and
> ...are usually served at dinner in, with or after the
> soup, fish or meats...and not, like fruits generally,
> as dessert.

John Nix, the New York tomato importer, had to pay. The Court's pragmatism was echoed in 1981, when the director of USDA's Division of Food and Nutrition Service officially declared that ketchup was a vegetable as part of the Reagan Administration's effort to justify cuts in the school-lunch program.

Fruit or vegetable—plant breeders have been changing the tomato ever since it cleaned up its reputation. Thousands of varieties have been produced, including the uniform cultivars that launched the Campbell Soup Company (which now sells more than 300 million cans of tomato soup each year). The latest breeding achievement—or mischief, some would say—is 'Flavr Savr', a commercial variety with tweaked genes developed by Calgene Fresh, Inc. Taking advantage of something known as antisense genetics, Calgene scientists were able to suppress the gene that controls softening. 'Flavr Savr' tomatoes ripen but remain firm, allowing commercial producers to delay picking.

What's next for America's favorite vegetable? The sky's not the limit, since the tomato—well, tomato seeds—were blasted into outer space in April, 1984. For six years, more than 12.5 million 'Rutgers California Supreme' seeds circled earth aboard a satellite, then were retrieved by the crew of the *Columbia*. Back on earth, the seeds were distributed to more than 3 million school children and 64,000 teachers in all 50 states, the District of Columbia and 34 foreign countries.

There are no rampaging killer tomatoes to report, though some recipients—an unrepresentative sample—suggested that space-exposed seeds germinated and initially grew slightly faster than earth-bound seeds, and that plants from space-exposed seeds had higher levels of chlorophyll and carotenes than the homebodies. Over time, however, the terrestrial tomatoes equaled their more adventuresome counterparts, and overall, no significant differences were found between the earthlings and the space travelers.

The experiments continue: SSE members are making third-, fourth- and fifth-generation NASA seeds available to home gardeners. And the seeds-in-space study, while it revealed no worrisome mutations, wasn't without casualties. "Dear NASA," wrote one participant. "My name is Matt. I am in grade 2. I really enjoy growing my plants. Here are my results. My earth seed did not grow. My space seed grew but it fell off my desk. It died."

TOMATO TERMS:
Or, What Is an F$_1$ Hybrid, Anyway?

BY KARAN DAVIS CUTLER

ARDENING BY MAIL is nothing new in this country, though service has improved since 1631, the year John Winthrop, Jr. spent weeks waiting while his seeds traveled aboard the *Lion* from England to the Massachusetts Bay Colony. Winthrop's order, which cost him £160, was heavy on vegetables and herbs, not flowers. Onions, parsley, carrots, parsnips, radishes, pumpkins, squash and cabbages were requested in greatest quantities. Cauliflower seeds were the most costly item in his 59-item order, which did not include tomatoes.

Today, tomatoes head every most-popular vegetables list, and mail-order seeds arrive in days, not weeks—or, for instant gratification, you can grab packets off a rack at the local nursery and have them in the ground 30 minutes later. But that doesn't mean buying has gotten easier. Packets often carry more abbreviations than contents, making many of us wish that seeds still came in cloth bags labeled simply BEANS or PUMPKIN. One tomato I ordered this year came "sealed for freshness" in a 3½-by-5-inch plastic-lined paper envelope bearing a color photograph of a seductive crimson fruit that could have only been produced in the Garden of Eden. The envelope reads:

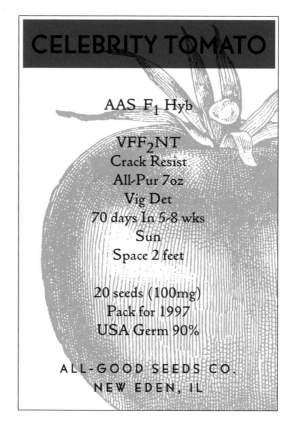

CELEBRITY TOMATO

AAS F$_1$ Hyb

VFF$_2$NT
Crack Resist
All-Pur 7oz
Vig Det
70 days In 5-8 wks
Sun
Space 2 feet

20 seeds (100mg)
Pack for 1997
USA Germ 90%

ALL-GOOD SEEDS CO.
NEW EDEN, IL

While it's tempting to ignore, even denounce this sort of horticultural shorthand, it's more useful to transcribe it. First off, the packet tells me that the cultivar of tomato I'm planting is 'Celebrity'. Plant cultivars, or varieties, are usually designated by single quotation marks. (There is a technical difference between a cultivar and a variety, the former a product of intentional breeding and the latter a result of accidental crossing, but the terms are often used interchangeably.)

Plants also have genus and species names (the tomato's is *Lycopersicon esculentum*), which are indicated by italics or underlining. The packet also tells me that 'Celebrity' is an **AAS**, or All-America Selections winner. It won in 1984, after being tested in AAS trial gardens throughout the United States, grown and compared with other tomatoes of its type and judged outstanding by independent horticultural experts.

Tomato plants are self-pollinating when left to their own devices (and desires), but the designation F_1 **Hyb** alerts me that 'Celebrity' is an intentional cross made between two distinct and stable, or "pure," tomatoes, using one as the male parent and the other as the female. Because 'Celebrity' is an F_1, or first-generation, hybrid, it should have better-than-average vigor and give me earlier, more uniform and higher yields. But seeds from my 'Celebrity' tomatoes won't produce 'Celebrity' tomatoes. I can save seeds for planting, but I'm unlikely to recognize—or like—next year's harvest.

In contrast to a hybrid like 'Celebrity,' an OP (open-pollinate, or non-hybrid) is a variety like 'Brandywine', a superbly flavored tomato selected by 19th-century Amish farmers who named it after a Pennsylvania creek. Most OPs result when someone, usually a home gardener, finds an unusual or clearly superior tomato, saves its seeds and plants them the next year. Then the gardener saves the seeds of the best fruits of the best offspring and plants again. And again and again. In time— five generations or more—the characteristics valued, such as size, flavor or hardiness, are stabilized, and seeds will produce plants and fruits that are identical to their parent. (According to Tim Peters, an Oregon vegetable breeder and seed-company owner, about 70 percent of tomato seeds will come true after three generations.)

In addition to coming true, OPs tend to be "locally adapted," suited to a particular region. They may have adjusted to the environmental conditions where they were developed or have multi-resistance to common diseases of their locale. For example, 'Tappy's Finest', a pink-red OP, does well in moderate to cool conditions like those in the West Virginia mountains where it originated.

Both 'Brandywine' and 'Tappy's Finest' are also heirlooms, OP varieties developed before 1940. (The first hybrid tomato, 'Burpee Hybrid', was introduced by the W. Atlee Burpee Co. in 1945.) While all heirlooms are OPs, not all OPs are heirlooms, for home gardeners and commercial breeders continue to develop new non-hybrid tomatoes, such 'Oregon Spring', an early, cold-resistant variety released by Dr. James Baggett at Oregon State University in the 1980s.

VFF$_2$NT tells me that 'Celebrity' plants are resistant—but not immune—to verticillium wilt, two races of fusarium wilt, nematodes and tobacco mosaic virus (for more information, see Protecting the Crop, page 43). Disease resistance, which breeders have developed in many new tomatoes, is crucial to gardeners who till infected soil or to those who live in regions, such as the South, where heat and humidity combine to support tomato diseases more vigorously than high-school cheerleaders support football teams. If your garden is packed with viruses, fungus diseases and other plagues, the more letters the better. The most resistant tomato would be something like AAsAnBCfClmCsFF$_2$GwLLbNNhrRknStSunTV (indicating at least some protection against *Alternaria* or early blight, alternaria stem canker, anthracnose, blossom end rot, catfacing, cladosporium leaf mold, crease stem, fusarium wilt race 1, fusarium wilt race 2, gray wall, septoria leafspot, late blight, root knot nematode, nail head rust, *Stemphylium* or gray leafspot, sunscald, tobacco mosaic virus and verticillum wilt). And it probably would taste like gauze.

'Celebrity' tomatoes resist cracking **(Crack Resist)**, a problem where rain falls unevenly and the soil's moisture flits from dry to soppy, or where rainfall is excessive. It is an all-purpose **(All Pur)** tomato—good for slicing on BLTs and into salads, making soup and canning—and a medium-sized variety, with fruits averaging seven ounces **(7 oz)**.

There are many ways to sort tomatoes, including plant size, fruit color (red, orange, pink, yellow, bi-color, other), maturity date (early-, mid-, late-season), use (all-purpose, salad, slicing, canning, paste/sauce, juice, stuffing), commercial or home varieties, hybrid or OP, but the most common method combines size, shape and use. From large to small, the usual classes are: beefsteak and/or very large, medium or standard, paste (plum and pear) and cherry.

'Celebrity' is a determinate **(Det)** tomato, the distant relative of a sport, or atypical plant, discovered in Florida in 1914. Compact and only moderately tall, determinates are bred to have a finite size. Once a determinate reaches its genetically programmed height, its stems produce terminal flower clusters that halt further stem growth. Like other determinates, fruits from 'Celebrity' ripen in a concentrated period, usually six weeks or less.

The tomato's wild progenitor is a viney plant that sprawls indefinitely. Anyone who has grown a vigorous indeterminate tomato like 'Sweet 100' can see firsthand the tomato's heritage (indeed, the world's record for "overall size" of a tomato plant is held by a cherry variety measuring 28 feet tall and 53 feet 6 inches wide). Indeterminate, in contrast to determinate, varieties continue to grow until they are halted by frost, and they produce earlier and more—and some argue better-tasting—fruits than determinates do. As long as the conditions are hospitable, indeterminate varieties will continue to set fruit.

Many determinates require no support, but 'Celebrity' is a semi- or vigorous determinate **(Vig Det)**, growing to 4 feet or so, and may need help to stay upright. In addition to vigorous determinates, there are dwarf determinates, such as 'Dwarf Champion' and 'Patio', which are small enough to grow in a 12-inch pot, and miniature determinates—'Minibel' is one example—which have tiny fruits, short stems and are most often grown in containers as ornamentals.

'Celebrity' is a mid-season variety—I should have ripe tomatoes **70 days** after the plants, which must be started indoors five to eight weeks **(In 5-8 wks)** before the frost-free date, are set in outside. If your season is long enough to sow tomato seeds directly in the garden, don't forget to add about six weeks to the days-to-maturity figure that appears on the packet as you calculate when you'll be picking your first tomato. 'Celebrity' plants should be located in full **Sun** and spaced 2 feet apart **(Space 2 feet)**. Large, indeterminate varieties, such as 'Sweet 100', may need as much as 4 feet between plants.

My packet contains **20 seeds**, which weigh 100 milligrams **(100 mg)**, or about 3/1000 of an ounce. If that doesn't sound like much, remember that one ounce of tomato seeds will produce about 9,000 plants. Barring disaster, six plants of a standard variety like 'Celebrity' should produce enough fruit for a family of four. If you want to can tomatoes or freeze sauce, double the number of plants.

The seeds in this packet were grown domestically **(USA)** and packaged for the 1997 garden season **(Pack for 1997)**. Most seeds packed for 1997 were grown in 1995, though they may have been grown

The horticultural shorthand on seed packets includes useful details, such as the plant's disease resistance, and whether it is a hybrid or an open-pollinate.

even earlier. Fresh seeds are always a gardener's best choice, but don't throw away leftover seeds. Tomato seeds remain viable five years or more. If you're using old seeds, test, or proof, them before you plant. Place a dozen seeds between damp but not soppy white paper towels. If six sprout, the germination rate is 50 percent, and you should buy new seeds; if the rate is between 65 percent and 85 percent, use the seeds but sow more thickly than usual. With **Germ 90 percent** listed on this packet, I can expect 18 of my 20 'Celebrity' seeds to sprout.

Finally, my seeds were packaged by **All-Good Seeds Co.,** located in **New Eden, Illinois.**

It's a headful of information, but my 'Celebrity' packet still doesn't tell how deeply I should sow or the ideal temperature for germination. How many days to germination? When do I transplant? What kind of soil, what pH, how much water and fertilizer? Will 'Celebrity' succeed in my region? Were the seeds treated with a fungicide; were they grown organically? What is the yield per plant?

No seed packet tells it all, nor does it have to. By law, a vegetable-seed packet need only include the species and variety names and net weight on its front side. Many states also require a packed-for-season declaration, the name and address of the packager and the country of origin if it is other than the United States.

But more tomato terminology is better than less. The envelopes to be avoided are the vaguely ones marked: **Easy to Grow Anywhere.**

Giant Red Tomato is not easy to grow anywhere. Trust me.

Don't believe it!

OFF & RUNNING:

Getting Started, Outdoors & In

BY SHEPHERD OGDEN

IT MAY COME AS A SURPRISE, but there are really only a few steps to growing great-tasting tomatoes. One is choosing the best varieties, and parts of this book (see pages 51-87) are devoted to helping you find those. But there are also a few tips and tricks that you can use to enhance the quality of your harvest, beginning with where you grow your tomato plants.

LAYING OUT THE GARDEN

Garden location is important, so choose your garden site with care. A spot close to the house—particularly the kitchen—is best. It discourages creatures from making midnight raids at the same time that it encourages you and your family to spend time in the garden, to stop often if only briefly to pull weeds, water or re-tie a wandering stem.

If possible, stay away from a "microclimate" that is particularly harsh for your area. In the North, this means avoiding low-lying, frost-prone areas that collect cold air on clear, still nights and northern slopes that hold their snow cover late into the spring; in hot, dry climates, the reverse is true—low spots on a gentle northern slope will require less water and will temper the effects of the sun during the hottest part of the year. The ideal spot—in most USDA zones—is one

Plant your garden in raised beds. The soil will remain loose and uncompacted, and you'll be able to double or triple your yields.

that receives full sun throughout the day, has protection from wind, has fertile, organically rich soil and is near a reliable source of water.

My first advice to new gardeners is, "Start small." The second thing I tell them is, "Plant in raised beds." Experienced gardeners know the folly of having a garden too big to care for, but many long-time gardeners still grow vegetables in widely spaced rows surrounded by bare ground. Keeping all that unused ground free of weeds requires extra cultivation and lowers productivity on a square-foot basis. If you have unlimited time and space, these may not matter much, but I've yet to meet the gardener who doesn't feel short of both.

If you plant your garden in wide, raised beds, which require two-thirds fewer pathways, you'll need less space to grow the same number of plants. You'll also be able to concentrate fertilizer and compost applications, and since the soil in raised beds rarely gets stepped on, it stays loose and uncompacted. As a result, you can double or triple your average yields.

By volume, productive garden soil is 25 percent air, 25 percent water, 40 to 45 percent minerals and about 5 percent organic matter. One of the basic principles of organic gardening is to feed the soil and let the soil feed the plants, so it's vital to get the soil into good condition.

Ideally, you should start preparing the garden a year ahead by cover-cropping the area. Cover-cropping means growing a vigorous, thickly sown crop of soil-improving plants, such as annual ryegrass or buckwheat, to choke out weeds. In spring, till or spade the cover crop in. If you suspect that your soil is depleted, spread compost or well-rotted manure and mix that in as well; if there is reason to believe the soil is highly acid or alkaline, do a pH test (simple testing kits are available at most garden centers). Tomatoes need slightly acid soil (pH 6.0-6.8).

Once the ground has been tilled or spaded in the spring, the only tools you'll need are a rake, shovel, marker string and stakes. Decide where the beds will be—run them from east to west—and then stretch string lines around stakes to mark the perimeter of the beds. The beds can be any size or shape you want, but their width should be determined by your reach: stoop down, reach forward and touch the ground with your outstretched hand. Don't make any bed more than twice that distance, and you'll be able to reach its center from the path on either side without straining. Length is less important, though I don't recommend making a bed more than 10 or 12 paces long so you won't have to walk great distances to get around to the other side.

Rake soil from the pathways outside the string onto the bed, layering the soil with compost. If your site has particularly poor drainage or thin topsoil, you can shovel additional soil from the path onto the beds, raising them even higher. After the beds are complete, mulch the paths with a thick layer of bark, sand, straw or cinders—whatever is suitable, local, cheap and responsible—to keep them weed-free.

If your garden is an established one, be sure to plant tomatoes where they or their family members, such as peppers and eggplants, haven't grown for at least four years. Tomatoes need rich soil that is not too high in nitrogen (N). Too much nitrogen relative to the available phosphorus (P) and potassium (K) will produce huge plants but few fruits.

GROWING SEEDLINGS

At our northern farm, we must grow tomatoes from transplants (if we planted from seed, the plants would be killed by autumn frosts long before the first fruits ripened). But don't be in a rush—a younger plant started later does better in the garden than one held too long on a windowsill. Similarly, a common mistake made by home gardeners who buy tomato plants is to purchase huge, spindly transplants complete with small fruits. Nothing could be worse, since once a plant begins to flower and form fruits, its

BUYING TOMATO PLANTS

- Buy only young, vigorously growing plants—avoid plants with flowers or fruits.
- Avoid tall, spindly plants—choose deep green plants that are as wide as they are tall.
- Check that plants are free of insects—be sure to look at the undersides of the leaves.

Transplant tomatoes a week after the danger of frost has passed. Set each plant deeply into the soil, up to within three or four branches from its top. A shovelful of compost and a handful of crushed eggshells worked into the soil will help provide essential nutrients.

most vigorous vegetative growth has passed. And the best-tasting tomatoes are the ones borne on plants with the most foliage per fruit.

I start tomatoes in plug trays six to eight weeks before the frost-free date, using a sterile, soilless potting mixture. Sow two seeds ¼-inch deep in each cell or pot and germinate at 75 to 80° F. Tomato seeds take between seven and 14 days to germinate (bottom heat will speed the process). Once the seedlings have grown their first true leaves—the ones with serrated edges—get rid of the weaker plant. (Cut rather than pull the reject so you don't disturb the roots of the seedling you're keeping.)

Now give the plants as much light as possible—a south window if you have one or, even better, artificial lights (set no more than three inches above the seedlings and keep the lights on at least 14 hours each day). If you're growing seedlings in your kitchen or living room, you may have to settle for the ambient temperature, but research has shown that you can increase the number of early fruits by exposing plants to a "cold treatment": allow the nighttime temperature to fall to 50° to 55° F for the first three weeks after thinning, but keep the temperature 65° or higher during the day.

Other secrets to success? Research shows that you'll produce more sturdy seedlings if you brush your plants. Twice a day, for one to two minutes, run your hand (or a piece of heavy paper) gently along the tops of the seedlings. If your seedlings are getting too large, install a small fan. Experiments by a Canadian researcher indicate that plants exposed to a slight breeze slowed their growth rate.

Fertilize weekly using seedling-strength liquid fertilizer, such as a liquid seaweed/fish emulsion mix (one ounce of each to one gallon water). As the

THE BASIC FOUR

The four most important plant nutrients for tomatoes are nitrogen, phosphorus and potassium—the N-P-K letters on bags of commercial fertilizers—and calcium (Ca).

NITROGEN is essential to leaf and stem growth. Good sources are well-rotted manure, compost, bloodmeal, fish emulsion and legume cover crops. Too much nitrogen produces large leafy plants but few fruits. Stunted growth and yellowing of lower leaves are signs of a nitrogen deficiency.

PHOSPHORUS promotes strong roots and the formation of flowers, fruits and seeds, and helps plants resist disease. Mined phosphate rock, bonemeal and poultry manure are excellent sources of phosphorus. Stunted plants with thin stems and leaves that have a purple cast on their underside are indications of a phosphorus deficiency.

POTASSIUM, contained in greens, granite meal and wood ashes, is important to plant vigor, growth and disease resistance. It leaches quickly, especially in light sandy soils, so add it in the spring when planting rather than in the fall. Stunted plants, poor yields and yellow-splotched foliage indicate too little potassium.

CALCIUM is crucial to the development of cell walls, especially in leaves, and to warding off blossom-end rot, a common tomato malady. Fluctuating or low soil moisture favors calcium deficiency. Natural sources include ground limestone, wood ashes and bonemeal; many gardeners add a handful of crushed eggshells to the planting hole of each tomato.

seedlings begin crowding one another, transplant them into larger and larger containers. Each time you transplant, bury the whole stem below the first set of leaves—tomatoes will send out roots from the buried stem—and by the time you set your plants outdoors, they'll have a strong root system.

MOVING OUTDOORS

Just as it's foolish to start tomatoes too early indoors, it's unwise to move them outdoors while the air and soil are still chilly. Tomatoes love warmth. Set them in frigid, wet soil and surround them with cold air and they'll languish. What's more, they won't survive if suddenly moved outdoors, where they must face sun, wind, rain and see-sawing temperatures. To prepare seedlings for these harsher conditions, they must be "hardened off," or acclimated. As planting day approaches, give them a chance to develop defenses by moving them outdoors for a few hours in the afternoon. Gradually increase the time they spend in the open air, until they are ready to face everything Mother Nature can throw at them.

While the seedlings are hardening off, prepare the bed by dumping a shovelful of compost where each plant will be set. I like to toss on a handful of crushed eggshells, too, to provide the extra calcium that tomato plants need. Compact varieties can be spaced as close as 2 feet, but large indeterminates need twice that much space. A week after the danger of frost is past and nighttime temperatures stay above 50° F and daytime temperatures above 65°, it's time to transplant. Incorporate the compost in a basketball-sized hole and set each tomato considerably deeper than it was growing in its pot—burying it up to within three or four branches from its top. The buried stem will send out extra roots, helping the plant take in the nutrients necessary for a bumper crop. Firm the soil and water lightly to remove any air pockets that may remain around the root ball.

Immediately after transplanting, I cover my tomatoes with floating row covers to protect them from wind, sun and temperature variations, and to keep out flying insects until the plants have established themselves. Many gardeners also set a cardboard tube around each stem to prevent cutworms from chomping seedlings off at the soil line. (Half a toilet paper tube works well and biodegrades.) After two weeks, I remove the row covers and set up whatever kind of support—cages, stakes, trellises—the variety requires (see "What's At Stake," page 35).

If you're pushing the season—trying to get tomatoes outdoors a bit earlier

CONTAINER TOMATOES

Landless gardeners can grow tomatoes as long as they have a sunny location protected from high winds. Breeders have created varieties especially for containers, such as 'Pixie Hybrid', 'Tiny Tim', 'Patio', 'Patio Prize' and 'Small Fry', but any variety will work if you remember that whatever it needs in a garden it also needs in a pot. (If your garden is a hanging basket, do choose a variety designed for that purpose, such as 'Toy Boy' or 'Tumbler'.)

Container tomatoes should be started, hardened off and transplanted on the same schedule as plants bound for the garden, with a few cautions:

• Use at least a five-gallon container (bushel baskets work well) that is wide as well as deep—tomato roots are shallow and need room to spread.

• Use a container with drainage holes and add several inches of pot shards or coarse gravel—don't place the container in a saucer.

• Use a fertile, slightly acid, humus-rich potting mix that drains well.

• Check soil moisture regularly—containers dry out quickly—and water thoroughly.

• Feed every two weeks with a balanced water-soluble fertilizer.

Water your tomatoes regularly to keep the soil evenly moist. After the soil warms up completely, mulch around the plants with straw, compost, dried grass clippings or other organic material.

than may be entirely wise—you should provide additional protection. Homemade shields include plastic milk jugs, rings of old tires and tomato cages circled with clear plastic. Or you can purchase commercial season extenders such as hotcaps or Wall O'Water teepees. But unless you live in a region with only 75 frost-free days, you're better off being patient—wait for the air and soil to warm up.

Once the transplants are well established in good soil, you're pretty much home free. After the soil warms up completely, mulch your plants with straw or dried grass clippings, and water regularly to keep the soil evenly moist. And keep dreaming about the season's first BLT.

IN THE GARDEN:

Keeping Things Growing

BY PAUL DUNPHY

O NCE I SET my young tomato plants in the ground, water them well and grace them with a benediction for fruitfulness, my mind takes a sabbatical of sorts and eagerly runs ahead of the season. My hands may be idly brushing soil off my pants, but my thoughts are skipping away through an imaginary calendar, scouting for signs of the first ripe fruit.

Ripeness in tomatoes cannot be figured to the hour, but it does arrive with a certainty, a brief shining moment unknown to potatoes, say, or carrots. The defining qualities of deep uniform color and firm flesh make it easy for me to focus my anticipation and, as the season unfolds, easy to compare the actual progress of my crop with the tomatoes in my neighbor's garden. As the most widely planted vegetable in North America, the tomato has become the standard for judging horticultural success.

Being the first in the neighborhood to pick a ripe fruit is fine. But as my familiarity with tomato culture has grown, I have come to realize that there are many different kinds of firsts, each its own reward. The first cherry tomato. The first medium-sized tomato. The first sauce. The first salsa. The first plate of sliced tomatoes and basil. The moment I most look forward to is picking my first heirloom beefsteak, my first 'Prudens Purple' or 'Brandywine'. I combine a single slice of the tomato with Jarlsberg cheese and fresh bread and take the sandwich

There are numerous techniques for encouraging early ripeness and, as importantly, for producing flavorful tomatoes that continue to bear long after the first fruit
has been harvested.

outside to eat in the same late-summer warmth that brought the fruit to ripeness. There are numerous techniques for encouraging early ripeness and, as importantly, for producing healthy, flavorful tomatoes on plants that continue to bear long after the first fruit has been harvested in triumph.

WATERING

Tomato plants thrive when their roots are deep in evenly moist soil. If the soil becomes parched, their growth slows and the fruit can become diseased. Dry spells can also lead to "cracking." In dry weather, fruit growth slows down and the skin slightly hardens. A heavy rain or generous watering can then bring a spurt of growth that splits the skin around the stem.

Tomato plants need at least an inch of moisture a week to ripen six or eight big fruits. Water your plants for a few minutes every day, if time allows, for the healthiest tomatoes.

Meanwhile, if the soil is always soggy, some delicate feeder roots are apt to die, curtailing the plant's ability to take in nutrients. To maintain soil moisture I often water around my plants for a few minutes every other day, if time allows, and increase the watering when the fruits begin to form. The plants need at least an inch of moisture a week to ripen six or eight big fruits which, after all, are mostly water.

Here is a simple formula for calculating the number of gallons needed to provide 1 inch of water to a given area: multiply the square footage of the garden bed by .083 (½ of a foot) by 7.5 (the number of gallons in a cubic foot of water). For a 100-square-foot bed this would be a little more than 60 gallons: 100 x .083 x 7.5 = 62.25 gallons. If you water by hand with the hose running at an average, comfortable rate, you will need about 20 minutes to put down 1 inch of water, or about five minutes four times a week.

A tomato plant is always drawing in water and moving it through its system, enabling it to absorb dissolved nutrients. One common tomato ailment called blossom end rot, characterized by dark leathery skin on the underside, or blossom end, of the fruit, is attributable to drought and the resulting inability of the plants to take up calcium. Dusting the garden in the fall with dolomitic limestone is one way to incorporate calcium in the soil. Keeping the soil moist will then help make the mineral available to the plants.

MULCHING

Several weeks into the season, after the soil has thoroughly warmed up, I like to spread an inch or so of compost around my plants as mulch. Straw or grass clippings will also do. The mulch discourages weeds and slows moisture loss from the soil. You can use almost any organic material, though some break down much more slowly than others. Among good mulches are alfalfa hay, buckwheat and cocoa bean hulls, grass clippings, leaves, pine needles and straw. Compost is my first choice, because it gives the plants more added nutrition as their fruits begin to size up.

Many growers, particularly in northern states and along the West Coast, cover their tomato bed with black plastic a few days before they set out their transplants. They then cut "Xs" in the plastic to set in the seedlings. The plastic not only gathers warmth to promote earlier fruiting, it also keeps down weeds. Some growers in southern states also use black plastic to get a jump on the season. However, as the season progresses, the plastic can gather too much heat and damage the formation of flowers and fruits. So by late spring, the plastic should be covered with an inch or so of organic material to insulate it from the sun.

Recent research has shown that tomatoes can be grown successfully in a mulch of hairy vetch. You sow the vetch seed in the late summer or fall, depending on your location. It will make slow growth through the winter in warm areas or resume growth in the spring in colder climates. A few days before setting out transplants, mow the vetch to a height of about 1 inch. Then push aside just enough of the stubble to set in your transplants and otherwise leave the mulch undisturbed. Not only does the vetch suppress weeds and conserve soil moisture, it makes nitrogen available to the tomatoes. Vetch is a leguminous plant that gathers nitrogen in nodules on its roots. Research has shown that, compared with black plastic, vetch markedly increases tomato yields, and it comes without the environmental costs associated with manufacturing and disposing of plastic.

FERTILIZING

Tomatoes are heavy feeders. If you begin with fertile soil, your plants may need little additional fertilizer as they grow and form fruits. Many gardeners—I'm one of them—rarely fertilize tomato plants during the growing season. But if your soil is suspect or your plants show signs that they need additional food (slow growth; small, pale or yellow foliage; foliage that is purplish on the underside), you should fertilize. Moreover, there is evidence that foliar sprays of fish emulsion improve yields and speed fruit development, and that high fertility helps plants cope with blight and other diseases. The best times to fertilize are a couple of weeks after transplanting, after the first flowers

Yellow foliage indicates a lack of nitrogen. If your plants show this or other signs of a nutrient deficiency, you should fertilize.

29

appear, when the fruits are the size of ping-pong balls and after you pick your first tomato.

Sidedressing with compost is an excellent way to give plants a nutritional boost. If more drastic measures are called for, you can ring each plant—be careful not to touch the plant stem—with a fairly balanced organic fertilizer, something in the 5-10-10 range. But don't overdo it: Charles Wilber, the current Guinness Book of World Record champion for producing the most pounds of tomatoes from a single plant—342 pounds of fruit from one 'Better Boy'—says that eliminating stress on plants, not heavy feeding, is the key to big yields. Above all, don't overdo the nitrogen: the result will be huge, lush plants and a dearth of tomatoes.

PRUNING

Tomato plants can be divided into two broad categories called determinate and indeterminate, and the amount of pruning and training you may want to undertake depends on which type you grow. Determinate varieties are relatively compact (their growth largely stops once the fruits form) so the plants need only a short stake or cage and little or no pruning. Indeterminate vines have growth points, or apical buds, at their tips, which will continue to grow as long as the weather remains warm and sunny. Because of their rambling nature, indeterminate types are commonly pruned and trained; otherwise, they will trail across several feet of garden.

There are a number of variations on the pruning theme. All of them are aimed at curtailing the growth of side shoots, or suckers, and encouraging the plant to put more energy into producing fruits. If you look at a tomato plant, you will see shoots emerging just above the joint, or axil, where a leafy branch meets the main stem. Unchecked, these shoots will bear leaves and flower clusters and eventually fruits. The problem for most gardeners is

Prune back the side shoots of indeterminate tomato plants for best fruit production.

that the growing season is not long enough for all these fruits to mature. By pruning out some or all of the side shoots, you reduce the fruit load and enable the plants to concentrate on the tomatoes forming on main branches.

To save seeds, scoop them out, place them in a jar with a tablespoon of water for a few days, then spread them out to dry on a paper towel or coffee filter.

HOME-GROWN SEEDS

Choose clean, slightly overripe fruits from vigorous, disease-free plants (remember that seeds should be saved only from open-pollinated varieties—seeds from hybrid cultivars will not produce plants equal to their hybrid parent). Halve each tomato, scoop out the seeds and pulp, place them in a small jar, and add one tablespoon of water. Allow the mixture to ferment—it takes between two and four days, depending on room temperature—stirring it several times a day. Pour off the liquid and spread the seeds on paper towels until dry, three to six days. (Or, halve each tomato, scoop out the seeds and pulp, and spread them on several layers of newspaper. When the mixture has dried, scrape the seeds off the paper, clean and store.) Tomato seeds should be stored only after they are completely dry. Label the seeds and place in a tightly covered container in a cool (45° F), dry location.

31

Some gardeners pinch out every sucker on the main stem to produce a tall thin plant that they tie to a stake or train to an overhead string (see "What's At Stake," page 35). Other growers leave one of the lowest sideshoots and train it to grow into a second main stem, so the plant has a U-shaped form. Still others take a more artful approach and let the sideshoots bear a few leafy branches, then break off the tip of each shoot before any flower clusters appear. This approach provides the fruits more protection against sunscald. It is also based on the belief that with more foliage, the plants can gather more sunlight and better formulate the rich interplay of sugars and acids that give tomatoes their sweet but astringent taste.

Lest these various techniques sound too demanding, I should note that a good many gardeners do no pruning at all. They support their plants with stakes or wire cages, then leave them to their natural inclination. As someone who has tried several approaches, I recommend that you experiment with pruning back the suckers on indeterminate plants, either all or part way, and see the effect on your crop. I expect you will be pleased. You can set pruned plants closer together, which will allow you to grow more varieties in a given space. And the fruits will be healthier and easier to find and will ripen earlier than on unpruned plants.

Even if you don't bother to shape your plants in this way, you can help your crop mature toward the end of the season by pruning off the fruit clusters that are still small and dark green and have little chance of achieving even a light green color on the vine. Do this three or four weeks before the first expected frost. Relieved of its juvenile fruits, the plant will direct its energy toward the larger, more promising tomatoes.

HARVESTING

The classic appeal of home-grown tomatoes is "vine ripening"—each fruit left on the plant until its color is an even glossy red (or yellow or orange or pink or purple), and its texture is soft but resilient. Pursuing perfection carries some risk that a fruit will slide past its prime and languish until its skin is dimpled and its taste insipid. So keep an eye on the bottom of the fruit. Tomatoes ripen from the blossom end. If the skin is losing any of its smoothness, pick the tomato right away, whether or not the shoulders are colored. This is especially true with large heirloom types like 'Prudens Purple', which can be overripe on the bottom before the shoulders become deeply colored.

As the summer lengthens and the crop begins relentlessly maturing, I pick any fruits that are within a few days of ripening. I know they will mature beautifully on the kitchen counter, beyond the reach of slugs or the risk of cracking.

When picking tomatoes, pay careful attention to the bottom or blossom end of the fruits, where they ripen first. If the skin of a tomato is losing any of its smoothness, pick it right away, even if the shoulders are not yet colored.

And they will be handy to give away—"Please, take some"—to any non-gardeners who happen by. Tomatoes ripen and store best at room temperature, out of the sun. If you put them in the refrigerator—and this is true of mature as well as immature fruit—they lose their flavor. The cold apparently stops the production of aromatic compounds.

There is little prospect that tomatoes left on the vine will ripen once daytime temperatures are in the low 60s. However, in many areas such cool temperatures do not settle in until a few weeks after the first frost. You can usually extend the season and coax some fruits toward ripening by using old bed sheets or spun-bonded fabric to cover the plants against early frosts. Keep the covers away from the fruits themselves to prevent the cold from damaging the skin. And remove the covers during the day.

When hopes for outdoor ripening fade, you can still enjoy fresh tomatoes by bringing the most promising fruits inside. To have a good chance of ripening, they should be in the "breaker stage"— pale green, with a blush of pink on the bottom. If the skin is pitted or mottled with dark spots, the tomato will probably decay before it ripens and should be tossed onto the compost pile. Dark green fruits should be enjoyed in sauce or piccalilli, as they are unlikely to ripen fully.

I wrap breakers in newspaper and set them on a shelf in the cellarway where the temperature runs between 60° and 65° F. Tomatoes that are closer to maturity go on the kitchen counter. Inevitably, some are lost to decay, but many of them brighten steadily like the dawn sky. The flavor of these late-ripening fruits is not as rich as those that matured under the summer sun, but in a late October salad their color alone is rewarding. (Some gardeners prefer to pull entire plants and hang them upside-down in a cool place—about 58° F—and pick the fruits as they ripen.)

As fall descends and frost blackens the viney skeletons of the tomato plants, I start cleaning up the beds by cutting off the vines just above the soil line and putting them in the compost pile. It takes some muscle to work a pair of pruners through the tough stems. It would be easier to pull the plants, but I want to leave the roots in the ground, where they will hold the soil through the winter. By spring, when I pull the stumps out, many of the delicate feeder roots will have broken down and added rich organic matter to the soil. I will not put tomatoes in that bed for three or four years to guard against soil-borne disease that could infect my young plants. And when I do plant them there again, I want the soil to be dark, fertile and disease-free, able to support another bumper crop of fruits.

WHAT'S AT STAKE:

Six Ways to Trellis Tomatoes

BY JANE GOOD

IF YOU'RE WONDERING whether it's necessary to stake your tomatoes, the answer is probably yes—depending on what you want. Supporting tomatoes is a trade-off that balances the sweetest, earliest, largest or most bountiful crop with the characteristics of the site, the growth habits of different varieties and your devotion to the process. Encouraging plants to grow up while growing up permits exposure to optimal amounts of sunlight, the effective use of space and easy accessibility for maintenance and harvest.

Trellised tomatoes can ripen up to two weeks earlier than those left to sprawl. Fruits that develop off the ground are cleaner and less prone to rot. Vines held aloft aren't as susceptible to ground-dwelling pests, such as slugs, or soil-borne disease organisms that splash up during rains or overhead watering. And in less-than-perfect conditions, plants perform better when offered a little protection and encouragement to reach for the sun and set their fruits high. (Only in areas where persistently strong drying winds prevail do tomatoes grow better if allowed to sprawl.)

Trellising is doubly advantageous in cool, partially shady places if plants are anchored to brick or stucco and thus can benefit from stored daytime heat. Tomato supports installed along walls exposed to direct sun also are useful for gardeners who want to get a jump on the season—but who are willing also to water vigilantly in summer when the reflected light and warmth may become intense. And quite apart from cultural concerns, trellised plants can add a decorative element to the garden.

Classified by growth habit, tomatoes are divided into two groups: bush, or determinate, varieties; and vining, or indeterminate, ones (see "Tomato Terms," page 14). With a few exceptions, you can trellis either type, but the amount of support and pruning required is a reflection of their differences. In general, determinate varieties need minimal support and pruning (see pages 30 to 32 for tips on pruning tomatoes). Whatever tomato you grow, whatever training method you select, here are four general cautions:

- Install your support system at the same time you transplant—tomato roots are shallow and may be damaged if you postpone installing stakes or other supports.
- Be sure your supports are firmly anchored and are strong enough for the plants they are to brace—a 4-foot-tall cage is inadequate for a 6-foot 'Sweet 100' plant.
- Don't put off until tomorrow what should be done today—trying to tie or thread large stems that should have been tied or threaded two weeks earlier is difficult at best, impossible at worst.
- Tie loosely but adequately—stems that are crushed by a too-tight twine or that fold over because they aren't supported sufficiently are stems that won't produce fruits.

There are dozens of ways to give tomato plants support. Here are the six best.

STAKING

Basic wooden stakes pounded a foot deep into accepting ground beside each plant are simple, reliable free-standing supports. To make them, angle-cut six-foot-long 2 x 2s or pickets. (Give heavy-fruiting plants additional support by fixing the stakes to a wall or adding guy wires.) After installation, loosely tie the stem as it grows to the stake with figure-8 loops of soft cloth strips or lengths of old stockings, sponge tube, horticultural ribbon, baling twine or raffia. Remove the stakes in the fall.

Staking is simple and inexpensive, but it requires both tying and pruning each plant to a single stem (or two stems, using two stakes). Such radical pruning will

Staking is simple and inexpensive, but it requires both tying and pruning each plant to a single stem (or two stems, using two stakes). Staking and pruning are especially suited to regions where rain is plentiful.

reduce your crop, but plants grown using one-stem staking take up less room, so the yield for a given space will be nearly the same as growing fewer non-staked plants. Staking and pruning are especially suited to regions where rain is plentiful; they're less appropriate in hot windy areas.

Because putting in individual stakes each year is time-consuming, some gardeners use heftier wood or metal posts that they leave in the same location for several years. Less work, yes, but be sure to monitor the area carefully, watching for signs of the ill effects that almost inevitably arise from not rotating crops regularly.

CAGING

Tens of millions of gardeners buy wire cages to support tomato plants. Cages are easy to install; growth is restrained within the cage; fruits are kept off the ground; and because little or no pruning is done, yields are higher than those of staked plants. Plants may require a little "threading" in the beginning—directing stray stems back inside the cage—but it is a chore that takes only a few seconds.

After one season, however, most gardeners discover that inexpensive commercial tomato cages are flimsy and inadequate for containing a good-sized plant. Enterprising growers have seized the benefits of this method by creat-

After one season, most gardeners discover that commercial tomato cages are flimsy and inadequate for containing a good-sized plant. It's easy to create sturdier homemade versions of the tomato cage. The best are 24-inch diameter cylinders of 6-inch square mesh wire bolstered with one or two stakes.

ing sturdier versions of the tomato cage, the best being 24-inch diameter cylinders of 6-inch square mesh wire (so you can reach through to pick the fruits), firmly pushed into the ground and bolstered with one or two stakes. For vigorous determinates, 3 or 4 feet tall is enough, but large indeterminate plants require cages at least 5 feet tall.

Cage variations include square wood structures—built to contain a single plant or a row or bed of plants—and stake-and-string cages (four 6-foot upright stakes encircled at 1-foot intervals with natural-fiber twine). Custom or commercial, metal, wood or twine, it's easy to turn a tomato cage into a mini-greenhouse that can be put in place on frosty nights and lifted on warm days. Simply drape a large clear plastic sheet over the dome or around the cage and secure it with clothespins.

Tomato trellises can be movable or permanent. If you opt for permanent wood structures, be sure to watch for diseases and other problems that arise when the same crop is grown in the same location for more than one year.

TRELLISING

For an instant trellis, fix a section of heavy-gauge 6-inch square mesh wire between two sturdy, well-anchored posts (height depends on the tomato variety you are growing). Set tomato plants at 18-inch intervals, install support posts between every two plants and, if necessary, add additional bracing to bear the weight of developing fruits as the season progresses. Each week, weave the young vines back and forth through the grid, taking care to remove most or all suckers. If your plants outdistance the trellis, encourage them to grow horizontally rather than vertically.

Six-inch-square nylon netting is less expensive than wire mesh, but it is difficult to remove the vines from the netting at the end of the season. Other gardeners train tomatoes on wood or bamboo trellises. If these are permanent structures like fences, be sure to watch for diseases and other problems that arise when the same crop is grown in the same location for more than one year.

Weaving is an effective and biodegradable way to support tomato plants pruned to two stems. At the end of the season, the plants as well as the heavy-duty natural-fiber twine used to secure them to anchor posts can be tossed on the compost heap.

WEAVING

Weaving, or basket weaving, is an easy, effective biodegradable method of supporting tomato plants that can be tossed en masse on the compost heap at the end of the season. Begin by placing anchor posts at each end of the tomato row; then drive additional stakes between every two plants. Once the plants—pruned to two stems—are 14 inches tall, run a line of heavy-duty natural-fiber twine 12 inches from the ground down the row, securing it to each post as you go. When you reach the end of the row, fasten the line and head back up the row, "enclosing" the plants between the twine. Add new strands at 8-inch intervals as the plants grow, weaving the stems between the horizontal strings.

Basket weaving is a favorite technique of commercial growers (who know it as "Florida Weave" or "San Diego Weave") because it is easy and inexpensive. To make the job go even faster, place the ball of twine on a stick for quick unraveling.

Another way to support tomatoes: stretch a heavy wire between two sturdy posts to build a simple stringing structure, keeping the plants pruned to a single stem. For a larger crop, add more vertical strings to accommodate two or three fruit-bearing stems per plant.

STRINGING

To use this method, set your tomatoes under a stable support (that is 1 foot taller than the ultimate height of the plants), such as a heavy wire stretched between two fence posts set at either end of the row. Firmly tie one end of a length of durable untreated garden twine to a short garden stake driven in at the base of the plant. Then, allowing about a foot of slack, loosely knot the other end of the twine around the overhead support. Keep plants pruned to a single stem by removing suckers. Each week, as the plant grows upward, gently guide the central stem around the twine, allowing at least one wrap for each flower cluster.

For a larger crop, add more vertical strings to accommodate two or three fruit-bearing stems per plant. If the plants reach the top of the trellis, cut back the central stem at one branch above the highest fruit cluster.

Propping plants horizontally is particularly effective in windy regions and places where tomatoes become diseased or damaged when left on the ground. One of the simplest props to build is made of 4-foot-wide concrete reinforcing wire cut to the required length, then arched over the new transplants.

PROPPING

Supports that allow tomato plants to sprawl off the ground—Quonsets and other horizontal frames—are more appropriate for vigorous determinates than for very tall varieties. While this technique takes up more space than staking, it is useful in windy regions, and in regions where tomatoes become diseased or damaged when left on the ground. Easy to install, these kinds of supports require little of the gardener beyond making sure that the plant stems emerge through the support.

There are many ways to provide horizontal support. One of the easiest is to make a sturdy Quonset from 4-foot-wide concrete reinforcing wire. Have the wire cut to whatever length you need—enough to cover two plants or an entire row—and then arch it over the new plants. It should be installed when the plants are transplanted; covered with plastic, the Quonset can double as a greenhouse while the plants are small.

An alternative prop can be made by laying a wooden trellis or concrete reinforcing wire parallel to the ground atop one-foot posts. Whatever mesh you install—wire, wood or fiber—be sure it and its supports are strong enough to bear the weight of mature plants and their fruits. ✦

PROTECTING THE CROP:
Natural Pest & Disease Remedies

BY BARBARA ELLIS

PESTS AND DISEASES don't have to stand between you and a bumper crop of tomatoes. Fortunately, tomatoes are relatively trouble-free, provided you take some basic preventive steps, prepare the soil well and give your plants a little TLC throughout the season. If problems still crop up, use the symptom-and-solution guide below to deal with them.

PREVENTION PAYS

Prevention begins with plant selection. If soilborne diseases such as verticillium or fusarium wilt have been a problem in your garden in previous seasons, choose resistant cultivars. A "V" after the variety's name indicates resistance to verticillium; "F" indicates fusarium resistance. Resistant cultivars are widely available for two other common tomato problems—tobacco mosaic virus ("T") and root knot nematodes ("N"). If you're not sure that any of these have been problems in your garden, see the guide below for symptoms.

Getting your plants off to a good start by preparing the soil and planting them properly will reduce or eliminate nutrient deficiencies, cold injury and other problems. Rotating your crops is another good pest- and disease-prevention tactic. Avoid

Tomatoes are relatively trouble free, provided you take some basic preventive steps. Inspect your plants every few days for signs of problems. Check the undersides of the leaves for pests. You may need to use a hand lens to detect tiny mites and aphids.

planting tomatoes where you have grown potatoes, peppers, eggplants or tomatoes during the past three to five years. These plants are related and are susceptible to many of the same pests and diseases. It's best to plant tomatoes after legumes, such as peas or beans, in your crop rotation scheme. Avoid planting tomatoes next to potatoes, too; early blight, a leafspot disease, can spread between the two crops.

As your plants grow, take time to inspect them every few days for signs of problems. Pick off any speckled leaves you see, which helps keep a variety of leaf spot diseases in check. Replenish the mulch as necessary and weed at least until the plants are large enough to shade out weeds. Look closely at the leaves for signs of insect damage or leafspot disease. Be sure to check under leaves for pests that hide there. (If you need bifocals for reading, wear them for checking plants! Otherwise you may miss pests like aphids and mites.) Keep an eye on the flowers to make sure they are setting fruit as they should. Use the guide below to determine if you see symptoms of a pest or disease that needs immediate treatment.

INSECTS

Insects are generally easier to recognize than diseases, although some of the pests that attack tomatoes cause disease-like symptoms. A hand lens is a useful tool to have for identifying some of the smaller pests that attack tomatoes, such as mites or aphids. Others, like cutworms, are easy to spot when they're at work but disappear entirely after their damage has been done. All the controls below are organic and are listed in order of least to most toxic.

PROBLEM: Seedlings severed at or below ground level.
CAUSE: Cutworms: night-feeding, ground-dwelling caterpillars that chew through stems.
SOLUTION: Push a 4-inch-long cardboard tube over seedlings at planting time. Or mix *Btk (Bacillus thuringiensis* var. *kurstaki)* with bran and sprinkle around seedlings as bait. Treating the soil with parasitic nematodes is also effective.

A "collar" placed around seedlings will deter cutworms.

Hornworms chew large holes in leaves and fruit. Pick them off by hand and drop them in a bucket of soapy water.

PROBLEM: Curled, puckered or distorted leaves that are yellow and covered with sticky honeydew. Clusters of pinhead-size insects, especially on or under new leaves.

CAUSE: Aphids: tiny, pale insects that suck plant sap.

SOLUTION: Blast these pests off the plants with a strong stream of water. Repeat this every few days, taking care to spray leaf undersides, until infestations are under control. For more serious problems, spray with an insecticidal soap or a pyrethrum/rotenone mix.

PROBLEM: Young leaves stippled with yellow or bronze and fine webbing spun under and between leaves.

CAUSE: Mites: tiny, spider-like insects that suck plant sap, causing dry spots on leaves or leaves that fall off.

SOLUTION: Mites are especially problematic during hot, dry conditions. Spray plants weekly with a strong stream of water to knock mites off the plants and create moist conditions that will discourage them. Or spray infestations with an insecticidal soap.

PROBLEM: Ragged holes chewed in leaves and/or holes chewed in green or ripe fruit.

CAUSE: Hornworms: large, 3 to 4½-inch-long green caterpillars with white stripes; and Colorado potato beetles: oval, orange-and-black-striped beetles (their larvae are orange with black spots). Both pests chew large holes or skeletonize leaves and can defoliate plants and chew on green fruit. Other caterpillars also attack tomatoes, chewing smaller holes in leaves or in fruits. Slugs and snails also chew tomato foliage and fruits, and leave characteristic slimy trails.

SOLUTION: Hand-pick hornworms or other caterpillars and drop them in a bucket of soapy water. (If hornworms are covered by white, rice-like pupae, leave them alone. The pupae are the cocoons of a beneficial parasitic wasp.) Spraying plants with *Btk* is also effective. For Colorado potato beetles, destroy the orange eggs, which are laid in neat clusters underneath the leaves. Hand-pick adults and larvae and drop them in soapy water. Or spray with *Btsd (B. thuringiensis* var. *san diego)*. Pyrethrum and neem are also effective. Hand-pick slugs and snails or trap them in shallow pans of stale beer.

PROBLEM: Tiny shotholes chewed in leaves.

CAUSE: Flea beetles: tiny black or brown beetles that jump when disturbed.

SOLUTION: Flea beetles are primarily a problem when they attack very small plants. Cover transplants with floating row covers at planting time to keep them at bay. For severe infestations, spray with pyrethrum or rotenone.

DISEASES AND CULTURAL PROBLEMS

Diseases can cause a baffling array of symptoms on both plants and fruits, and to complicate matters even more, cultural problems can cause disease-like symptoms. But don't despair. Most often, once you determine whether you're dealing with a disease or a cultural problem it's fairly easy to choose the right control measures. Use the following guides to symptoms and solutions to identify and solve these problems organically.

PROBLEM: Yellowed, wilting leaves at the bottom of the plants followed by wilting stems or entire plants. Plants may be stunted.

CAUSE: Various diseases, including verticillium or fusarium wilt, root knot nematodes, Southern bacterial wilt. Verticillium and fusarium begin at the bottom of the plant, but eventually the entire plant wilts and dies, even with adequate soil moisture. The plants may be stunted, and stems may have a discolored layer when cut open. Root knot nematodes stunt plants and cause them to wilt in hot weather, even when well watered. Roots of afflicted plants will have gall-like knots or swollen sections. Plants attacked by Southern bacterial wilt go limp while the leaves are still green and do not recover when watered.

These malformed fruits are edible. To prevent catfacing, protect plants from extreme temperatures.

Blossom end rot can be caused by too much nitrogen, a calcium deficiency or uneven moisture.

SOLUTION: There is no cure. Destroy any plants afflicted by these problems—and do not add the diseased plants to the compost pile. Plant resistant varieties in future years and be sure to rotate their location. Applying parasitic nematodes to the soil can help control root knot nematodes.

PROBLEM: Spots on leaves or fruit. Spots on leaves may be yellow, watersoaked, brown or papery. Spots on fruits may be green and watersoaked, or raised and tan or scabby. Spots on leaves or fruits may have concentric rings and be large or small. Or, leaves may be mottled with yellow and borne on plants with distorted stems.

CAUSE: A variety of fungal, bacterial and viral diseases cause these symptoms.

SOLUTION: Destroy plants that have distorted growth and leaves that are mottled with yellow, as these are symptoms of tobacco mosaic virus. For other symptoms, pick off affected leaves and discard them in the trash, not the compost pile. A fruit with small spots is generally edible, but use it promptly. To prevent the spread of these diseases, spray plants with a copper-based organic fungicide. Spraying transplants with an antitranspirent can also be effective. If problems are extensive, have your local Extension Service identify the particular disease involved; resistant or tolerant cultivars are available for several of these diseases.

PROBLEM: Seedlings shrivel or rot at soil line and fall over.

CAUSE: Damping off—this fungal disease rots through stems at the soil line.

HELP BY MAIL

The following companies sell organic pesticides, traps and other products for controlling diseases and pests.

Earlee, Inc.
2002 Highway 62
Jeffersonville, IN 47130

Gardens Alive!
5100 Schenley Place
Lawrenceburg, IN 47025

Harmony Farm Supply and Nursery
3244 Highway 116
Sebastopol, CA 95472

Necessary Trading Company
P.O. Box 305
New Castle, VA 24127

Peaceful Valley Farm Supply
P.O. Box 2209
Grass Valley, CA 95945

SOLUTION: Prevention is the only solution—once damping off attacks, there is no cure. Before you sow seed, disinfect seedling containers with a 10 percent chlorine bleach solution several hours to one day before planting. Let containers dry, then fill with sterile potting medium. A dusting of milled sphagnum moss or vermiculite over the top of the soil surface is helpful. Provide seedlings with good air circulation and light, and water them from the bottom. Thin seedlings to prevent overcrowding.

PROBLEM: Malformed, cracked or blotched fruit. Fruits may crack open to expose the interior flesh, be catfaced and gnarled, black and rotted on the blos-

Yellowed, wilting leaves at the bottom of plants may indicate fusarium wilt.

som end, or marred by large, off-color blotches.

CAUSE: Various cultural conditions can cause these problems. Fruits on plants grown in soil that fluctuates widely from dry to wet often crack open. Black, rotted spots on the bottom or blossom end of a fruit indicate blossom end rot. This can be caused by damaged roots, too much nitrogen in the soil, a calcium deficiency in the soil or drought or uneven soil moisture, which can prevent the plant from taking up calcium. Catfacing is caused by cold temperatures when the plants are flowering and fruits are forming. Sunscald, which causes pale or grayish blotches on the fruits, is the result of inadequate leaf cover.

SOLUTION: In general, all these problems can be handled by providing plants with optimum growing conditions; afflicted fruits are generally edible. Providing evenly moist soil through the season is paramount, as is protection from cold temperatures. Good care will also help prevent leafspot disease, which can cause leaves to drop, exposing the fruits to the sun and scalding. If blossom end rot is a recurring problem, have your soil tested for calcium and add high calcium lime as recommended by the test. Gardeners in hot, sunny regions may want to plant tomatoes in light shade and to prune judiciously (or not at all) to prevent sunscald.

PROBLEM: Fruits fail to form.
CAUSE: Various cultural causes can impede fruit set. Temperatures that exceed 90° F or that dip below 50° F will cause flowers to drop without forming fruit. Drought causes flowers to drop and plants to be stunted. Excess nitrogen in the soil will cause plants to grow lush leaves at the expense of fruit.
SOLUTION: When temperatures moderate, plants will begin setting fruit. Try cold- or heat-tolerant cultivars if extreme temperatures are a common problem in your area (cherry tomatoes are often less affected by heat). Keep the soil evenly moist throughout the season. Avoid high-nitrogen fertilizers.

IN EXTREMIS:

Coping with Difficult Climes

GROWING TOMATOES IN THE SOUTHWEST

BY AURELIA C. SCOTT

THE SOUTHWEST'S DESERT CLIMATE presents tomato-loving gardeners with a unique combination of challenges, including perpetual drought, low humidity, burning sun and incessant wind. The soil is alkaline and salty, mostly sand in some regions, largely clay in others. During the growing season, moisture comes only in the form of brief afternoon thunderstorms or hailstorms.

This catalog of depressing details is enough to make even a certified Master Gardener think twice before spending $1.50 on a packet of 'Early Girl' seeds. But we Southwesterners are a hardy and inventive bunch. We have discarded many tomato-growing techniques recommended for most parts of the country and

The author's garden. Southwesterners must adopt a unique set of gardening practices to overcome perpetual drought, low humidity, burning sun and incessant wind.

adopted special practices for gardening in our low and high desert regions. We've learned to protect tomato plants from daytime heat and sun, irrigate efficiently, shelter plants from moisture-robbing wind and turn much-less-than-ideal soil into a version of loam. Here are some tips for fellow desert dwellers who want to grow tomatoes.

SOIL & SITE

• Build 5-inch-high, double-dug raised rows or beds that have been enriched with compost or other organic material. Site the beds to run north to south, which will give the plants an east-west exposure.

• Provide filtered shade by planting tall sunflowers or trellising vines on the south side of the garden (in USDA Zone 9, provide shade on the west side as well). Or plant tomatoes on the east side of the garden, where they can receive early morning sun but are sheltered by corn or other tall crops from strong afternoon rays.

• Dig compost or other organic matter into the garden several times a year. This is essential. Humus reduces the salinity of southwestern soil; it improves the water-holding capacity of sandy soil and aerates clay soil; and it helps alkaline soil release nutrients to the roots of plants.

SEEDS & PLANTING

• Select short- or midseason tomato varieties, which flower before daytime temperatures reach the 90s and set fruit better in the Southwest's cool nights. Choose tomatoes that have disease resistance, especially to early blight, which sometimes infects large areas of the Southwest; generally, however, diseases and insects are not much of a problem in this dry, hot region.

• Direct Seeding: In the hottest, driest regions (USDA Zones 8 and 9), direct seed in January and February for a summer crop; direct seed in late July for a fall crop. Bury the seeds ½- to 1-inch deep, mulch lightly and water well. Be sure to secure the mulch to keep it from blowing away.

• Indoor Seeding: Sow seeds indoors five to eight weeks before transplanting into the garden. In USDA Zones 8 and 9, transplant seedlings from late February to mid-April for a summer crop; transplant seedlings in late August for a fall crop. In Zones 5, 6 and 7, transplant seedlings from early April to mid-May. (Do not delay transplanting once the danger of frost is past: tomatoes will not set fruit once the daytime temperatures reach 95° F.)

• Allow seedlings to adjust to sun and wind by hardening them off before transplanting them into the garden.

• Choose seedlings that are thick-stemmed and at least 8 inches tall.

• Transplant seedlings in the late afternoon to help protect them from bright sun.

• Plant seedlings deeply, burying at least half of the plant; water generously and mulch with about an inch of organic matter.

TOMATOES FOR THE SOUTHWEST

'Beefmaster': meaty, very large fruits; prolific indeterminate vines; disease-resistant

'Burbank Red Slicing': 6- to 8-ounce fruits; compact plants; drought-resistant; heirloom

'Celebrity': prolific new standard determinate variety; disease- and crack-resistant

'Early Girl': standard early-season variety; bears well in heat and cold

'Marvel Striped': large, juicy, pleated orange and yellow fruits; vigorous plants require trellising

'Prize of the Trials': tasty orange cherry; good variety for hot dry climates

'Red House Free Standing': juicy 6-ounce fruits; heat tolerant; compact plants with dense foliage

'Roma VF': meaty paste variety for cooking; compact vines

'Sweet 100': prolific, vigorous vines with 1-inch fruits; vigorous indeterminate

'Yellow Pear': pear-shaped, 2-inch-long non-acid fruits; indeterminate; heirloom

'Roma' plum tomatoes are a good choice for the Southwest. They make a good meaty paste for cooking, and grow on compact vines. Like other tomatoes grown in the region, they should be fertilized when transplanted and again when they begin to bloom.

• Immediately protect the new plants from wind with a floating row cover made of a spunbonded fabric, such as Reemay, Agronet or Tufbell, or with cages wrapped with spunbonded fabric.

TENDING

• If growing bushy determinate varieties, you may leave the plants to sprawl on the ground. If space is limited or you are growing large indeterminate varieties, cage or trellis the tomato plants as they grow. Staking, with its necessary pruning, exposes the plants to sun and wind and leaves them vulnerable to cool overnight temperatures. It is not recommended for Southwestern gardeners. Nor is heavy pruning, which exposes the fruits to the Southwest's worst garden foes: intense sun, wind and hail. Not pruning helps the plants to shade themselves during the day and to retain warmth at night.

• In regions where nighttime temperatures regularly drop below 55° F, wrap the bottom half of each cage with horticultural plastic or a spunbonded fabric.

• Dry, alkaline soil ties up nutrients—feed transplants with a balanced fertilizer when you set them out and again when the plants begin to bloom.

• Water with drip or soaker hoses, or by flooding the furrows between the raised rows. Avoid overhead watering. It is wasteful, wetting only the top few inches of the soil, raising salts from the subsurface and crusting lightly mulched soil.

• Saturate the soil with water two or three times during the growing season to flush out salts.

- In sandy soil, water established plants deeply (until the soil is wet to a depth of 8 inches) once a week, if the soil is clay, water deeply every 10 to 12 days. Always water deeply: shallow watering increases soil salinity in the root zone, which can damage plants.
- Never leave the soil uncovered. Apply at least 2 inches of organic mulch under mature plants. Unless gardening high in the mountains, do not use plastic mulches.

GROWING TOMATOES IN THE SOUTH

BY PAT STONE

THERE ARE TWO PROBLEMS with growing tomatoes in the South. One is heat. That may sound strange to gardeners in cold zones, who can hardly get enough warm weather to ripen a tomato. But too much, as always, is too much. When daytime temperatures climb above 85° F, or night temperatures above 75°, tomato plants have trouble setting fruit.

There's not much a gardener can do about the weather, though breeders have tried to come to the rescue by developing varieties, such as 'Atkinson', 'Sunmaster' and 'Bonus', which can set fruit and flourish in hot weather. Partial shade for plants may help some, but the best strategy is to accept reality and plan so that your plants set fruit before and/or after that absolutely hottest time of the year. Of course, that varies depending on where you live: some gardeners in south Florida have their best harvests in December! And acceding to the weather is not such a tragic loss for Southerners, who can still harvest homegrown tomatoes for a longer time each year than people in most sections of the country.

The other problem, blight, is more serious. Blight is part and parcel of growing tomatoes in the South. To put it another way, I never have to worry about frost killing my plants—they don't last that long.

Blight is the bane of tomato growers in the South. Early blight is shown above. Varieties resistant to early and late blight are available, but they aren't necessarily the most flavorful tomatoes you can grow.

To double our problems, blight comes in two forms, early and late. Early blight, also known as alternaria stem canker (from *Alternaria*, the fungus that causes it), first appears on stems and older leaves. It can be ruining your foliage without destroying all the fruit, so you may still get some harvest. There are a good many tomatoes with early blight resistance, but for my money, the best are the "Mountain" series of tomatoes—'Mountain Fresh', 'Mountain Supreme', 'Mountain Pride' and 'Mountain Belle'—developed by Randy Gardner, an agricultural researcher at North Carolina State University's Mountain Horticultural Crops Research Station. One caveat: tomatoes bred to fight blight are not necessarily the most flavorful varieties a home gardener can grow.

Late blight is caused by the *Phytophthora* fungus and makes its presence known by a white downy mold that appears on plant leaves. It strikes like a forest fire—in three days, your plants can go from green to black. Late blight is harder to fend off than early blight, and breeders have done less work on developing resistant varieties. 'Floradel', 'Southland', 'New Hampshire', 'New Yorker', 'Surecrop', 'West Virginia' and 'Nova' lay claim to late blight resistance, and according to Randy Gardner, the "Mountain" series show "some" resistance to late as well as early blight.

Blight spores can come by wind, water and insect, and they overwinter in plant debris. Even dew transmits early and late blights, so they're pretty much unavoidable in the humid South. The determining factors for how bad the blights will be are heat and, especially, humidity. During a dry summer, blight won't be a bad problem. During a wet one—Whoa, Nelly!

FIGHTING BLIGHT

There are a slew of strategies for avoiding or reducing blight infestations.
- Rotate your plantings of tomatoes and their kin, such as eggplant and potatoes, and remove all spent plants from the garden.
- Make sure your tomatoes get plenty of sun and ventilation (don't plant them too close together; thin the foliage if need be).
- Spray plants with compost tea (high fertility produces new foliage) and with a homemade solution of one teaspoon baking soda per quart of water as a fungal preventative.

TOMATOES FOR THE SOUTH

'Arkansas Traveler': late-season southern heirloom with pink fruits; good heat-tolerance

'Better Boy': more hardy hybrid son of 'Big Boy', which conquered the South like Sherman when it was introduced in 1949; large crop of red fruits on large indeterminate vines

'Brandywine': no disease resistance, but many Southerners consider this potato-leafed indeterminate heirloom the best-flavored tomato of them all

'Dad's Mug': indeterminate red heirloom with deep creases for stuffing or paste—a novelty number for the tomato show

'Mountain Supreme': standard red determinate tomato from Randy Gardner with outstanding resistance to early blight

'Ozark Pink': indeterminate 5-foot pink variety from the University of Arkansas; bred for hot, humid regions

'San Marzano': pear-shaped, bright red paste heirloom excellent for processing; indeterminate

'Solar Set': new determinate variety from University of Florida, which sets fruit at higher temperatures than most varieties

'Sunmaster': midseason determinate variety known for its heat tolerance; sets fruit best in high temperatures

'Sweet Million': tiny cherry tomatoes that make for good grazing; indeterminate hybrid with great flavor and yields

The "Mountain" series, including 'Mountain Fresh', 'Mountain Supreme', 'Mountain Pride' and 'Mountain Belle', are among the best tomatoes bred for resistance to early blight.

- Mulch around the bases of tomato plants to eliminate soil splash. Clip off blighted foliage (dip your shears in a baking soda solution between cuts to clean them).
- Set out successive plants to stave off early blight, which attacks older foliage.

These ploys may help avoid blights, or slow their spread. But I know of only two real controls. One is to spray your plants with copper-based fungicide, such as copper sulfate or Bordeaux, as soon as you spot the telltale signs. The big problem with this tactic, assuming you don't mind using toxic substances in the garden (even natural products like these), is that you have to be relentless. You must spray every 7 to 10 days and after every rainfall.

The second ploy is to keep your tomato foliage *utterly* and *absolutely* dry. In other words, roof your plants. Grow tomatoes in a greenhouse, if you have one, opening or removing its sides so it doesn't overheat. Water plants from below, using drip irrigation or some other method that keeps water from splashing on the foliage.

No greenhouse? Set your plants under an overhang, or grow container plants on a porch. Two summers ago, every tomato vine in my garden was felled by blight before I picked a single fruit. But the plant I grew in a barrel under my house's front overhang? It was still bearing in September. Moral: when it comes to blight, absence (of leaf moisture) makes the fruit grow fonder.

GROWING TOMATOES IN THE FAR NORTH

BY LINDEN STACIOKAS

T HE COOLER AND SHORTER GROWING SEASON, frigid soil and filtered sunlight of northern climes used to restrict gardeners there to greenhouse tomatoes. However, the last few years have seen a proliferation of varieties—many first imported by Bill McDorman, owner of Seeds Trust/High Altitude Gardens in Idaho, from the coldest regions of the former USSR—that do well outdoors despite arduous growing conditions. By planting these new tomatoes and by using special techniques, gardeners in even the coldest places can grow respectable fruits. Not the stuff of legends, but darn nice tomatoes.

In very cold climates you can compensate for slow-to-warm-up soil by laying the tomato plants horizontally in 6-inch-deep troughs. The root and about half of the stem should be covered with soil amended with compost.

In the Far North, young tomato plants need to be protected from frigid June winds.

Tomatoes are warm-weather plants, preferring air temperatures of 70° to 85° F during the day, 60° to 70° at night. Soil temperatures, too, are crucial to steady growth. The ground at northern latitudes can be considerably colder than the 60° usually considered the minimum for producing tomatoes. Raised beds and mulching the garden with clear plastic are two techniques cold-climate gardeners use to increase soil temperatures.

For years, I struggled with hilled rows that eroded over the course of summer. I finally rebuilt my plot: now it consists entirely of wood planters that are 5 feet wide, 4 feet tall and 10 feet long. In early April, I push the snow off the soil and cover each bed with 6-mil. clear plastic, which warms the soil more effectively than colored plastics. By May, the soil in the planters is 10° to 15° warmer than the dirt in the surrounding yard. The clear plastic remains anchored over the containers until the day of planting, in order to take every advantage of the sun.

While all this activity is going on outside, indoors I am sowing seeds. The ground will not be warm enough for seedlings until June 1, but the more mature the transplant, the earlier the harvest. So in early April, I sow tomato seeds in flats filled with a moistened commercial soil mix and seal them under a tent of clear plastic wrap.

As soon as half the seeds sprout, I whisk off the plastic cover and place the flats under grow lights, which I keep on 16 hours a day. I water only when the soil is dry to the touch and feed every ten days with a liquid fertilizer high in phosphorus. (Soils in interior Alaska tend to be phosphorus deficient, which explains why 10-52-10 is our most popular fertilizer; phosphorus also hastens maturity, an eternal consideration among northern gardeners.) After about a

A clear plastic mulch warms up the soil more effectively than colored plastics. To take every advantage of the sun, don't remove the clear plastic until the day of planting.

month, I transplant the seedlings to larger quarters, using cut-down milk cartons as pots. I set each seedling slightly deeper than it was previously growing, and water with a diluted high-phosphorus liquid fertilizer. About two weeks before the plants go outdoors, I begin hardening them off. Seedlings exposed to steadily increased doses of sun, wind and cool air develop leaves and stems that are better able to cope with outdoor conditions once they go into the garden to stay.

OUTDOOR TECHNIQUES

Despite raised beds and plastic mulch, the soil in my garden at transplant time is often still so cold that it adversely affects plant development. I compensate by employing trench planting: I dig troughs, 6 inches deep, and fill them half-full with compost; then I lay each plant horizontally (the root and about half of the stem) in the trough, and cover with soil. (The same frigid ground that can stunt plant growth also keeps our drinking water an icy 39°, so I use the hot-water tap when plants need additional moisture.)

Every transplant—they're now about 14 inches tall—is immediately given a wire cage lined and capped with 6-mil. clear plastic. These act as miniature greenhouses, gathering heat and blocking the frigid June winds. Other garden-

ers I know use hotcaps—either purchased or homemade from plastic milk jugs—or pile old tires around each plant. The plastic is removed—but the cage left to provide support against our brisk winds—in early July, when I apply more compost. The compost is meant to supply nutrition, but it also acts as a moisture-retaining mulch. (Since organic mulches delay soil warming, they should not be laid down in the spring in far-north gardens.)

It usually frosts the third week in August, so whatever fruits are still green are left on the uprooted vines, which I hang upside down in the base-

TOMATOES FOR THE NORTH

'Celebrity': one of the largest tomatoes we can raise in the Far North

'Galina's': flavorful cold-climate variety from Siberia; 1-inch yellow cherry fruits

'Golden Nugget': small, juicy yellow fruits that are virtually seedless

'Husky Gold': lovely orange-yellow fruits, about 6 ounces; sweet flavor

'Oregon Spring': compact, early maturing determinate; 4-ounce fruits with few seeds and sweet flavor

'Sasha's Altai': very early Russian variety and a good producer; juicy fruits with a real tang that some find too sharp

'Siletz': nearly seedless large fruits; rich flavor but not sweet

'Stupice': Czech variety; very early and good flavor; potato-leaf foliage

'Tanana': Alaska-bred determinate; heart-shaped fruits with a sharp taste that not everyone likes, but reliable and prolific

'Willamette Pink Cherry': extremely early; 1-ounce, low-acid pink fruits

ment. Even in the best years, I only get to eat about 40 percent of the fruits straight from the garden. Harvesting 60 percent of the tomato crop from the cellar may discourage most gardeners, but those of us who live in cold climates find a special sweetness in biting into a ripe basement tomato while watching an early September snowfall.

GROWING TOMATOES ON THE PACIFIC COAST

BY ROSALIND CREASY

TOMATOES ARE LIKE GOLDILOCKS. Most varieties like it not too hot, not too cold, but just right. But I garden in northern California, near the Pacific Ocean, and not in a fairy tale. Tomatoes here can only dream of just-right conditions as they languish in 50° nights and under foggy morning skies. If I plunk large or late-season varieties in my garden, where the sun arrives at noon, my reward is a meager crop of small, tasteless fruits.

I endured a decade of meager crops of small, tasteless fruits before I tapped into the experience of other area gardeners and began experimenting in my own garden. Learning to adapt to local conditions and choosing appropriate varieties—as well as a little serendipity—led me to tomato success. I now grow good-sized crops of delicious-tasting fruits. And I can proudly say that some years I even harvest what my 10-year-old neighbor Sandra Chang calls "truly awesome" tomatoes.

Gardeners living where summers are cool must learn two great lessons in growing tomatoes. First, we must resist the temptation to buy giant beefsteak varieties, which need near-perfect conditions to pollinate and take what seems like years to mature. Instead, we must choose tomatoes that are adapted to cool conditions, such as many of the early varieties, the small- and medium-sized salad types and the cherry varieties. And second, we must provide as much extra heat to the plants as we possibly can.

'Quick Pick', a reliable, disease-resistant, cool-tolerant hybrid, is a good bet for the Pacific Coast. The plants produce meaty 5-ounce fruits.

Because of our difficult conditions, local newspaper columnists give almost weekly guidance for growing tomatoes. I've tried many of their suggestions, including the use of floating row covers; milk-jug cloches; water-filled plastic bottles circled around young plants; staking; and black plastic mulch. All these heat-increasing techniques helped.

I've had help choosing varieties, too. Our area is blessed with a dynamic Extension Service agent and an active Master Gardener program. Together, they run tomato trials and then hold "taste tests" at the county fair. The flavor winners are almost always early or cool-tolerant varieties, such as 'Early Girl', 'Stupice' and 'Quick Pick'. 'Sweet 100' and other cherry tomatoes do well; and one larger tomato, 'Better Boy', gets good marks in the warmer parts of the county. Interestingly, some varieties that are touted for doing well in cool conditions don't score well on flavor: 'Siberia' and 'San Francisco Fog' produce good-looking fruits but have consistently been judged tough and tasteless.

CHANGING CIRCUMSTANCES

All this information plus my own trials paid off: every year, I harvested more and better tomatoes, though they were cherry or small-fruit varieties. Then a new problem emerged: the shade from my neighbors' trees forced me to move my vegetable beds from the back yard to the front. In upscale suburbia, this was a new ball game. The bleach-bottle cloches were tacky, the row covers looked like sleepers at a sorority slumber party. I am a champion of edible landscaping—and a designer of edible landscapes. My garden had to produce tomatoes *and* be beautiful.

By happy circumstance, I decided to install a little "secret garden" for my neighbor Sandra. We converted a sunny portion of the front yard along the heat-absorbing asphalt driveway to an enclosed garden, 12 feet by 24 feet. The fence was made from 6-foot wood posts and concrete reinforcing wire. Inside the

TOMATOES FOR THE PACIFIC COAST

'Better Boy': popular home variety that sets fruit in wide temperature range; large, sweet fruits

'Brandywine': heirloom famous for its flavor; worth trying except in coolest areas

'Dona': French hybrid with outstanding flavor; early indeterminate

'Early Girl': long-time favorite for its reliability, productivity and flavor

'Golden Mandarin Cross': Japanese variety with superb flavor but marginal in cool climates

'Oregon Spring': adapted for cool climates; 6-ounce fruits with good flavor

'Quick Pick': my most reliable tomato; hybrid with excellent disease resistance; meaty 5-ounce fruits

'Enchantress': disease-resistant, hybrid paste variety—wonderful for cooking

'Stupice': very early Czech cultivar with good flavor

'Sweet 100': unending crop of wonderfully sweet cherry fruits; must be staked and pruned

fence, we built raised beds enriched with humus to help drain the adobe soil and flagstone paths to absorb still more warmth. We tied each tomato plant to an 8-foot redwood stake to keep it off the cool soil, and pruned the plants so more sun could reach the fruits.

Sandra, of course, wanted BIG red tomatoes in her garden, so we started two BIG tomatoes, 'Better Boy' and 'Brandywine', indoors in early February in order to have 16-inch plants to set out early in May. Unlike cold-climate gardeners, I'm not waiting for frost-free weather to transplant. I'm waiting for daytime temperatures that are reliably in the 60s and soil temperature above 50° F. To hedge against failure, we also started three old reliables: 'Early Girl', 'Quick Pick' and 'Sweet 100'.

To my surprise—and both my and Sandra's delight—we produced fabulous beefsteak tomatoes. The fence, which we covered with beans and cucumbers, kept out the wind; the flagstones and driveway trapped heat; and—here's where the serendipity comes in—we had a warm summer. 'Brandywine', in particular, lived up to its reputation as one of the tastiest tomatoes in existence. The fruits are big and sweet with a velvety, juicy texture and intense tomato flavor—the kind of flavor that makes people look skyward and close their eyes in thanksgiving.

Sandra wanted BIG beafsteak tomatoes in her secret garden, above. Thanks to a wind-blocking trellis and a serendipitously warm summer, she got them.

I won't have spectacular beefsteak tomatoes every year—it's just too cool here—so small-fruit varieties will continue to top my seed list and the seed list of most Pacific Northwest gardeners. But Sandra and I will cross our fingers and plant the giants. The secret, after all, was in the secret garden.

PICK OF THE PATCH:
The Experts' Choices

O MATTER HOW GOOD the grower, a tomato bred for greenhouse culture is unlikely to succeed in a northern New York backyard. There are many tomatoes—'Celebrity' is a good example—that do well throughout the country, but seasoned gardeners learn to match the variety with the region. What follows are the choices and comments of 20 tomato-growing experts. Their experience will help you choose a variety right for your garden.

UNION, MAINE   USDA ZONE 5

Garden columnist A. Carman Clark, who is working on a mystery with a gardener protagonist, has strong drying winds in her rocky hilltop farm in southern Maine. She averages 140 frost-free days a year, but only about 100 days are warm enough for growing tomatoes. To get water to plant roots, she buries two-quart containers with drainage holes among her tomatoes.

'Sungold'

CLARK'S CHOICES:
'**Sungold**': small, sweet and prolific— "I fill my pockets with these on the way to the pond and share them with 70+ swimmers"

'**Super Tasty**': new from W. Atlee Burpee, this good-tasting red hybrid is early and plants are bushy, ideal for small gardens

'Siletz'

'**Early Girl**': perfect for tomato sandwiches—earliest indeterminate with high yields late into the season

'**Siletz**': extra-early productive indeterminate with 6-ounce red fruits

'**Celebrity**': one of the best new tomatoes—good flavor and disease resistance

GREENSBORO, VERMONT   USDA ZONE 3

Lewis and Nancy Hill have written a small library of garden books (the latest is *Bulbs: Four Seasons of Beautiful Blooms),* run a nursery and still find time to grow tomatoes. Earliness is essential when choosing tomato varieties for a northern Vermont garden—they average only 80 frost-free days—and a 15-foot deer-and-moose fence is their most important horticultural equipment.

THE HILLS' CHOICES:

'**Cabot**': firm, medium-size bright red fruits—low, compact plants that need little support

'**Early Girl**': good-size fruits with good flavor—plants do best when staked and heavily pruned

'**Pilgrim**': compact, heavy-bearing plants—fruits are uniform, well flavored and crack-resistant

'**Scotia**': dwarf plants but productive—medium-size red tomatoes touched with green when ripe

'**Cherry Cascade**': hybrid cherry with clusters of small fruits—the earliest tomato we grow

COLD SPRING HARBOR, NEW YORK USDA ZONE 7

Garden photographer/author Cathy Wilkinson Barash—her most recent book is *Edible Flowers*—usually grows tomatoes in containers filled with compost and potting soil rather than in the clay-loam of her Long Island garden. Pot or ground, she can count on 180 frost-free days each year.

BARASH'S CHOICES:

'Sungold': small, golden orange tomatoes with great taste; these ripen well when picked green at the end of the season

'Taxi': early yellow variety with medium fruits and strong tomato flavor—juicy yet firm

'Super Sweet 100': bite-size hybrid tomatoes with excellent flavor—wonderful in salads—large plants

'Purple Cherokee': dusty pink heirloom with superb flavor and consistency—and green shoulders

'Olympic Flame': lovely looking fruits—red with orange flaming—large, indeterminate plant

'Taxi'

NEW PALTZ, NEW YORK   USDA ZONE 4

Horticultural consultant Lee Reich is the author of several gardening books, including *Uncommon Fruits Worthy of Attention* and *The Pruning Book*. Reich gardens in southern New York, where he averages 130 frost-free days annually. His soil is silt loam, heavily amended with compost.

REICH'S CHOICES:

'Giant Belgium': indeterminate plant with low yields and ugly dark pink fruits, but they are very large and delicious

'Sungold': sweet-tart flavor, beautiful persimmon color—so good they rarely make it to the kitchen

'San Marzano': for sauce and canning only—simply the best-tasting cooking tomato

'Carmello': round, medium-size red French hybrid—disease-resistant indeterminate vines produce large crops

'Dona': reliable early red hybrid from France—big, disease-resistant plants

WARFORDSBURG, PENNSYLVANIA USDA ZONE 6

Market gardener Cass Peterson has 150 frost-free days to mother the 100-plus tomato varieties she plants at Flickerville Mountain Farm & Groundhog Ranch. Over time, she's discovered that high fertility—foliar feeding with fish emulsion—is the most successful treatment for the early blight encouraged by eastern Pennsylvania's wet spring weather.

PETERSON'S CHOICES:
'Jetstar': the best standard red tomato—hybrid, early, reliable, good-tasting and season-long production
'Pineapple': large heirloom tolerant of weather stress—sweet fruits have marbled red-yellow flesh, a crowd-pleaser at the market
'Arkansas Traveler': medium-size heirloom with pink skin, red flesh and excellent flavor—heavy producer all season
'Sungold': small, tangerine-orange

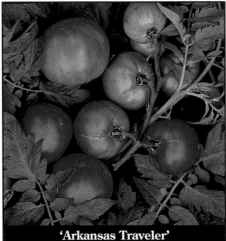

'Arkansas Traveler'

cherry—"the sweetest tomato I grow and a great kid favorite"
'Sausage': meaty, banana-shaped heirloom for sauce and canning—very large plant

GREENSBORO, NORTH CAROLINA USDA ZONE 7

The editor of *Carolina Gardener* magazine, L.A. Jackson gardens in north-central North Carolina. His soil is clay, "amended with beaucoup compost," and his site is sunny, which helps offset the humid summers. Despite a 200-day growing season, he uses an artificial tomato pollinator, which helps "plants produce earlier, more meaty fruits."

JACKSON'S CHOICES:
'Early Girl': always a consistent performer and easy to find in garden centers
'German Johnson': big, meaty heirloom with potato-leaf foliage and ol' time flavor—pink-red skin and few seeds
'Cherokee Purple': an ugly heirloom tomato—it's the color of a bruise—but excellent flavor

'**Sungold**': pretty bright orange cherry tomato with bet-you-can't-eat-just-one flavor

'**Celebrity**': medium-size determinate variety; so prolific that two plants will fill the refrigerator

PITTSBORO, NORTH CAROLINA   USDA ZONE 7

Small-scale market grower and garden writer Deborah Wechsler has 180 frost-free days to cultivate her central North Carolina "silty clay loam." Her garden "is in a clearing surrounded by trees. There's plenty of sun, but air circulation is poor, so disease resistance is important in choosing tomato varieties here."

WECHSLER'S CHOICES:
'**Better Boy**': dependable main-crop hybrid—large, tasty red fruits.
'**Celebrity**': hybrid with excellent disease resistance—good producer and good flavor
'**Sungold**': outstanding vigor, productivity, flavor and disease resistance—the best yellow cherry tomato
'**Sweet Million**': best of all the small-fruited red cherries—good crack-resistance and superb flavor
'**Sweet Chelsea**': best of the larger cherry tomatoes—bears well even in hot, humid weather

'Early Girl'

CHAGRIN FALLS, OHIO   USDA ZONE 5

Susan McClure, author of *The Harvest Gardener* and *The Herb Gardener,* has 150 frost-free days to grow tomatoes in the clay soil of northeastern Ohio. To check disease problems created by high humidity, she spaces plants widely to ensure good air circulation and mulches to reduce splashing.

MCCLURE'S CHOICES:
'**Big Rainbow**': late but worth the wait—huge, sweet heirloom with yellow flesh streaked with red

'**Celebrity**': reliable in the worst weather—medium-size, disease-resistant fruits

'**Sweet 100**': very vigorous red cherry—wonderfully sweet flavor

'**Husky Gold**': good-flavored yellow tomato that continues to produce long after other tomatoes have quit

'**Brandywine**': no disease resistance but flavor so superb that it's worth trying—does best in dry years

'Brandywine'

HUNTSVILLE, ALABAMA   USDA ZONE 7

Garden trouble-shooter Barbara Pleasant *(The Gardener's Weed Book, The Gardener's Bug Book, The Gardener's Guide to Plant Diseases)* has 210 frost-free days in her northern Alabama location. She gardens in red clay, "improved with horse manure and work," and grows huge crops of tomatoes despite high humidity and "all the soil-borne tomato diseases."

PLEASANT'S CHOICES:

'**Sweet Chelsea**': mid-size cherry that is vigorous, trouble-free and full-flavored

'**Sungold**': small, orange-yellow cherry that is prolific in hot weather—looks great in salads

'**Early Girl**': mid-size slicer—the first to ripen, yet has a truly long season

'**Enchantment**': hybrid, egg-shaped salad tomato—the best all-purpose red tomato around

'**Park's Whopper**': hybrid indeterminate; "it's the most flavorful large slicer"—20 fruits per plant in a good year

CHILLICOTHE, ILLINOIS   USDA ZONE 5

Bookseller Keith Crotz, proprietor of American Botanist, grows tomatoes in north-central Illinois, where the "clay soil is better suited for pottery than gardening." His 120-day growing season is characterized by high temperatures and humidity. To keep diseases at bay, he mulches with newspapers and straw.

CROTZ' CHOICES:

'**Garcia's Cherry**': very big cherry tomato—golf-ball size—that is meaty and sweet

'**German Johnson**': fine reddish pink variety that resists blossom end rot "despite our heavy soil"

'**Brandywine**': huge red heirloom that tastes like the tomatoes Grandma grew

'German Johnson'

'**Dad's Mug**': a deep red, ox-heart-shaped variety with good flavor and yields—very large plants

'**Georgia Streak**': large, indeterminate bi-color heirloom; orange and yellow inside and out, with great flavor but slightly seedy

DOWNERS GROVE, ILLINOIS   USDA ZONE 5

Master Gardener Bill Aldrich, founder and editor of *Chicagoland Gardening* magazine, has a 160-day growing season in his northeastern Illinois garden. His suburban vegetable plot is shaded in the late afternoon, but rich loam soil is some compensation for not quite enough sun.

ALDRICH'S CHOICES:

'**Brandywine**': deep red color and incredibly complex, sweet flavor—plants susceptible to disease but usually hold their own

'**Cherokee Purple**': sweet beefsteak with outstanding flavor—dark red-purple color

'**Celebrity**': vigorous determinate with mid-size fruits that are uniform and fine tasting—excellent for slicing

'**Sweet 100**': very sweet taste—fruits so abundant that one plant is enough for a family

'Big Beef'

'**Big Beef**': hybrid beefsteak with beautiful large, round fruits—and flavor that balances sweet and acid

KINGSTON, ONTARIO   USDA ZONE 5

Ken Allan, amateur breeder, seed seller and writer *(Sweet Potatoes for Northern Gardens)*, tills heavy clay in his southern Ontario garden, where he averages 110 frost-free days. He uses clear plastic mulch to speed soil warming in spring and advises that "no tomato is fully ripe until several days after it turns red."

'Elberta Girl'

ALLAN'S CHOICES:
'Sweet Million': hybrid cherry with superb sweet-acid flavor—large indeterminate plants
'Fantastic': good standard tomato—highly productive, with excellent flavor
'Brandywine': less productive than many varieties but rich fruity flavor makes up for smaller yield
'Nepal': large, deep red fruits with outstanding flavor—productive with some disease resistance
'Ultra Magnum': compact indeterminate beefsteak variety with a Brandywine-like flavor

BOVEY, MINNESOTA   USDA ZONE 3

Master Gardener and freelance garden writer Margaret A. Haapoja has been gardening in sandy lakeside soil in northern Minnesota for 25 years. Surrounded by forest, her garden receives less than eight hours of sun daily and often requires watering; to help cope with a 95-day growing season, she prunes the tips of her plants beginning August 1.

'Evergreen'

HAAPOJA'S CHOICES:
'Early Cascade': high-yielding early variety with small-to-medium fruits produced in grape-like clusters
'Early Girl': early, dependable variety with perfectly shaped, medium-sized fruits
'Floramerica': widely adapted mid-

season tomato, productive and disease-resistant—large fruits

'Imur Prior Beta': small, salad-size indeterminate variety from Norway "the first to ripen in my garden"

'Supersonic': vigorous determinate that produces large, crack-resistant fruits—developed for upper Midwest and New England

CALAMUS, IOWA   USDA ZONE 4

High-school science teacher and free-lance writer Glen Drowns cares for a 3½-acre vegetable garden in eastern Iowa, where there are 160 frost-free days a year. His soil is sandy, requiring big applications of organic matter every year, and summers are humid, which often leads to blight problems.

DROWNS'S CHOICES:

'Hawaiian Cherry': high-yielding, superbly sweet tiny cherry variety—tall plants with lush foliage

'Evergreen': medium-size sweet tomato with excellent sweet flavor; rare variety; remains green when ripe

'Hungarian Italian': the best of the paste tomatoes—high yields, determinate, thick meaty fruits

'Garden Peach'

'Garden Peach': excellent keeper—heirloom with large, red or yellow, low-acid fruits with fuzzy peach-like skin and blush

'Elberta Girl': beautiful striped fruits with fine flavor—plant has ornamental dusty miller-like foliage

DALLAS, TEXAS   USDA ZONE 7/8

Stacy Reese, a county agent for the Texas Agricultural Extension Service, has a nine-month growing season but is plagued with heavy clay soil, high winds in spring and drought in summer. To compensate, he uses raised beds, waters with a drip-irrigation system and "always chooses disease-resistant varieties."

REESE'S CHOICES:

'Carnival Red': determinate variety with good disease resistance—larger fruits than its sister 'Celebrity' and more compact plants

'**President**': vigorous determinate with excellent disease resistance developed for the home garden—6-ounce fruits

'**Celebrity**': outstanding main-crop tomato with multiple disease resistance—medium globe-shaped red fruits

'**Superfantastic**': improved disease-resistant version of 'Fantastic'—midseason highly productive hybrid indeterminate with 10-ounce fruits

'**First Lady**': extremely early hybrid indeterminate—disease- and crack-resistant mid-size fruits

ALBUQUERQUE, NEW MEXICO   USDA ZONE 7

Cooperative Extension Service horticultural specialist George Dickerson has a 173-day growing season characterized by strong sun, high temperatures and little rain. Tomatoes growing in his sandy loam soil, which he covers with a black plastic to retain moisture and discourage weeds, must be watered twice weekly.

'Super Sweet 100'

DICKERSON'S CHOICES:

'**Celebrity**': plants have excellent disease resistance—fruits flavorful and well shaped

'**Early Girl**': still one of the best early varieties—good tasting and productive

'**Super Sweet 100**': best of the cherry tomatoes—heavy producer but has a tendency to crack

'**Delicious**': very good, large, red tomato—indeterminate vine that should be pruned for better yields

'**Better Boy**': favorite home-garden hybrid; large red tomato with good disease resistance and foliage protection against sunscald

SANTA ANA, CALIFORNIA   USDA ZONE 10

Bill Sidnam spent 20 years as a garden columnist for the *Los Angeles Times;* he now writes for the *Orange County Register.* His southern California location is subject to strong Santa Ana winds from fall to early spring. But he also has 365 growing days a year, so he can plant tomatoes as early as February and as late as August.

SIDNAM'S CHOICES:
'**Champion**': large red fruits with great flavor—indeterminate hybrid that keeps producing even in adverse conditions
'**Better Boy**': produces large red fruits over a long period of time—indeterminate hybrid with disease resistance
'**Celebrity**': reliable producer of quality red fruits—determinate that sets fruits in all climate zones
'**Early Girl**': very early producer—4-ounce red tomatoes with excellent flavor and resistance to cracking
'**Momotaro**': new pink tomato from Japan—superb flavor

CORVALLIS, OREGON   USDA ZONE 8

Biologist and plant breeder Alan Kapuler is research director for Seeds of Change, where he specializes in developing high-nutrition vegetables. In his western Oregon garden, spring lasts from January to June and summer until November, giving him more than 225 days to work his clay-loam soil.

KAPULER'S CHOICES:
'**Peacevine Cherry**': tresses of ¾-inch red tomatoes with excellent flavor and productivity—highest vitamin C content of all cherry varieties
'**Stupice**': very early Czechoslovakian variety with outstanding flavor—3- to 6-ounce red fruits with potato-leaf foliage.
'**Double Rich**': productive midseason slicing tomato—2-pound red fruits bred for high vitamin C content
'**Caro Rich**': dark orange, mild-flavored fruits that are higher in beta carotene, the precursor of vitamin A
'**Red Currant**': different species *(Lycopersicon pimpinellifolium)* with tiny fruits in grape-like clusters—intense, sharp, acidic flavor

MONROE, WASHINGTON   USDA ZONE 8

Part-time market gardener and newspaper columnist Mary Schultz is also a co-curator for Seed Savers Exchange. She raises more than 400 different vegetable varieties each year in her Pacific Washington garden, including 100 tomatoes, which are difficult to grow in her cool, cloudy, windy region despite fertile loam soil and an average of 210 frost-free days.

SCHULTZ'S CHOICES:

'Moonglow': huge orange fleshy fruits with almost no seeds—exceptional taste

'Yellow Wendy': very large Australian indeterminate salad variety—clusters of ping-pong ball-sized fruits that are deliciously sweet

'Taxi': round yellow 6-ounce fruits with great sweet taste—slight determinate plants that do well in cages

'Sausage'

'Oregon Spring': early, red, seedless 8-ounce fruits, "the closest we can get to a beefsteak tomato in the Pacific Northwest"

'Sausage': vigorous determinate paste variety—unbelievable yields of solid sausage-shaped fruits

ANCHORAGE, ALASKA   USDA ZONE 3

Jeff Lowenfels, garden columnist for the *Anchorage Daily News,* has been gardening in southern Alaska for 25 years, long enough to know that "moose like a good tomato." He has 110 frost-free days annually, but cold nights and winds force him to choose varieties that set fruit at low temperatures.

'Sub Arctic 25'

LOWENFELS' CHOICES:

'Sub Arctic 25': sprawling plants with red 2-ounce fruits—a reliable producer in Alaska

'Siberia': one of the earliest tomatoes, it can set fruit at 38° F—abundant clusters of red, 3-ounce fruits.

'Glacier': cold-tolerant tomato with small fruits and unusually good flavor for an ultra-early variety

'Early Tanana': Alaskan tomato—small plants, small-to-medium red fruits that are slightly pointed on the blossom end

'Wilamette Pink Cherry': almost the first tomato of the season—low acid but good flavor.

ONE TOMATO, TWO TOMATOES:

A Guide to Cultivars

BY KARAN DAVIS CUTLER

IF YOU BUY TOMATO PLANTS at the local garden center, the choices are manageable; but if you start from seed, the possibilities are mind-boggling. James McFerson, a scientist with the USDA-ARS Plant Genetic Resources Unit, Cornell University, Geneva, New York, estimates that there are about 40,000 *Lycopersicon esculentum* accessions held in genebanks worldwide, 10,000 in the United States alone. Redundancy is high, according to McFerson, bringing the real number closer to 25,000.

How many are available to you? McFerson's guess is somewhere between 1,000 and 2,000, which excludes USDA-ARS holdings, as these are usually only made available to researchers. The latest edition of Seed Savers Exchange's (SSE) Garden Seed Inventory—a list of commercially available, open-pollinated vegetable varieties—lists nearly 550 tomatoes. Through SSE, a nonprofit organization devoted to preserving open-pollinated vegetable varieties, you can obtain hundreds of non-commercial varieties as well—with names like 'Olga's Yellow Round Chicken', 'Roughwood Golden Plum', 'Box Car Willie', 'Grandmother Oliver's Green', 'Heart of the Bull', 'Dixie Golden Giant', 'Grandpa's Cock's Plume' and 'Egyptian Tomb'. By joining SSE, you become part of a network of gardeners from whom you can obtain seeds of these hard-to-find tomatoes.

Gardens are finite, however. What follows are 75 outstanding tomatoes, all available commercially (see page 101 for Additional Resources). Some are well-known, some less familiar. This is a place to start, but don't limit yourself: seeds for 'White Rabbit', 'Ding Wall Scotty', 'Chalk's Early Jewel', 'Yellow Tommy Toe' and 'Nebraska Wedding' are waiting to be planted. Who could resist?

'Abraham Lincoln': I; OP; beefsteak; L; red; heirloom
Solid 12-oz. fruits; bronze-green foliage; slow to ripen

'Arkansas Traveler': (F); I; OP ; standard; M/L; pink; heirloom
Irregular 6-oz. fruits; good for South, sets fruit in heat; prune for larger fruits

'Beefsteak': I; OP; beefsteak; L; red
Meaty, faintly ribbed 1-lb. fruits; classic beefsteak variety

'Bellstar': D; OP; paste; M; red
Large plum from Canada; firm, meaty 4-oz. fruits; good canner

'Better Boy': (VFNAs); I; H; standard; M; red
Widely adapted; large crop of 12-oz. fruits; fine flavor; good leaf cover

'Big Beef': (VFF2AsLsNT); I; H; beefsteak; M; red
Good flavor, meaty 10-oz. fruits; exceptional disease resistance; widely adapted; AAS winner

'Big Rainbow': (AAs); I; OP; large; L; multicolor; heirloom
Green-red-yellow 1.5-lb. fruits; needs long season to mature

'Brandywine': I; OP; standard; M/L; dark pink; heirloom
Traditional Amish variety widely considered best-tasting tomato available; rough 10-oz. fruits; no disease resistance; potato-leaf foliage

'Burgess Stuffing': I; OP; stuffing; L; red
Large, hollow bell pepper-like fruits; mild flavor

'Carmello': (VFNT); I; H; standard; M; red
French market favorite; large crop of 8-oz. fruits; widely adapted

'Caro Rich': D; OP; standard; M; orange
High vitamin A content; low-acid 5-oz. fruits; does well in cool climates

'Celebrity': (VFF2AsNLsT); VigD; H; standard; M; red
Widely adapted; 7-oz. globe-shaped fruits; heavy yields; outstanding disease resistance; AAS winner

'Delicious': I; OP; beefsteak; M; red
Round, smooth 1-lb. fruits; improved form of 'Beefsteak'; holds record for world's largest tomato (7 lbs. 12 oz.)

'Dona': (VFF2NT); I; H; standard; M; red
French home-garden favorite; glossy, fine-flavored 6-oz. fruits

'Floramerica'

'Doublerich': D; OP; standard; E/M; red
Bred for high vitamin C content; firm 4-oz. globe-shaped fruits; high yields; good canner

'Earliana': I; OP; standard; E; red; heirloom
Green-shouldered 4-oz. fruits; mild flavor; popular in West

'Earlirouge': D; OP; standard; E; red
Home and market variety; 6-oz. fruits; widely adapted

'Early Girl': (V); I; H; standard; E; red
Rich-flavored 4-oz. fruits; reliable home-garden favorite; high yields (more disease-resistant form available)

'Evergreen': I; OP; standard; M; green; heirloom
Meaty 4-oz. fruits that are green when ripe; sweet mild flavor

'Floramerica': (VFF2NLsAs); D; H; standard; E/M; red
8-oz. fruits; excellent disease resistance; AAS winner

'Giant Belgium': I; OP; beefsteak; L; dark pink; heirloom
2-lb. low-acid very sweet fruits

'Glacier': VigD; OP; standard; E; red
Bred for cool regions; 2-oz. fruits with good flavor; high yields

'Green Zebra'

'Green Grape': VigD; OP; cherry; M/L; yellow-green
Clusters of 1-inch bi-colored fruits with green flesh; sweet-tart flavor

'Green Zebra': I; OP; standard; M; striped
Slightly ribbed 3-oz. fruits striped green and yellow; mild-flavored green flesh

'Heatwave': (VFF2); D; H; standard; E/M; red
Tasty uniform 8-oz. fruits; heat-tolerant variety suited for Southeast

'Homestead 24': (FAs); VigD; OP; standard; M/L; red
8-oz. fleshy, uniform fruits; bred for hot, humid climates; do not prune

'Husky Gold': (VF); I; H; standard; M; yellow-orange
Mild, sweet 7-oz. fruits with orange flesh; AAS winner (red and pink forms
also available)

'Hybrid Ace': (VFN); D; H; standard; L; red
Disease-resistant hybrid version of 'Ace', a commercial variety;
mild-flavored 6-oz. fruits; adapted for West

'Ida Gold': D; OP; standard; E; orange
Bred for cold regions; low-acid 2-oz. fruits; productive throughout season

'Jetstar': (VF); I; H; standard; M; red
Firm, meaty, low-acid 8-oz. fruits; high yields; does best when staked and
pruned

'Lemon Boy'

KEY

I – indeterminate
D – determinate
Vig – vigorous
OP – open pollinate
H – hybrid
E – early (up to 65 days)
M – midseason (66-79 days)
L – late (80+ days)

DISEASE RESISTANCE:

A – alternaria (early) blight
As – alternaria stem canker
F – fusarium wilt, race 1
F2 – fusarium wilt, race 2
Ls – gray leafspot
N – nematodes
T – tobacco mosaic virus
V – verticillium wilt

'Lemon Boy': (VFN); I; H; standard; M; yellow
Mild-tasting, 7-oz. globe-shaped fruits; widely adapted

'Marglobe': (F); VigD; OP; standard; M; red
Popular old home and commercial variety; sweet 6-oz. fruits; susceptible to cracking

'Marmande': (VF); VigD; OP; standard; E/M; red
French "gourmet" variety; 5-oz. irregular, flattened fruits; large yields; grow in cages

'Moretown Hybrid': (V); I; H; standard; M; red
7-oz. meaty fruits; rich flavor; good canner; Northeast favorite

'Mortgage Lifter': (VFN); I; OP; beefsteak; L; red
Improved form of Southern heirloom 'Radiator Charlie's Mortgage Lifter'; sweet 1-lb. fruits

'Mountain Pride': (VFF2AsLs); D; H; standard; M; red
Smooth 7-oz. fruits; disease-resistant "Mountain" series bred for hot, humid regions

'New Yorker': (VAs); D; OP; standard; E; red
Commercial variety; concentrated crop of 5-oz. fruits; good cool-weather variety

'Oxheart'   'Persimmon'

'Northern Exposure': D; H; standard; E/M; red

Bred for short, cool seasons; large crop of 8-oz. fruits

'Oregon Spring': (V); D ; OP; standard; E; red

Adapted for regions with short, cool summers; 6-oz. seedless, globe-shaped fruits

'Oxheart': I; OP; large; L; rose-pink

Fleshy, mild-flavored 1-lb. heart-shaped fruits; do not prune ('Yellow Oxheart' also available)

'Ozark Pink': (F); I; OP; standard; E/M; pink

7-oz. mild fruits; good variety for hot, humid regions

'Peacevine Cherry': I; OP; cherry; M; red

¾-inch fruits with highest vitamin C content of all red cherry varieties

'Persimmon': I; OP; standard; L; orange; heirloom

Globe-shaped 14-oz. fruits; persimmon-colored; fine distinctive flavor

'Pilgrim': (VFF2ALs); D; H; standard; M; red

Firm, crack-resistant 7-oz. fruits; adapted for cool, short summers

'Pixie': D; H; cherry; E; red

1¾-inch fruits; excellent flavor; compact 16-inch plants suited to container growing ('Orange Pixie' also available)

'Quick Pick'

KEY

I – indeterminate
D – determinate
Vig – vigorous
OP – open pollinate
H – hybrid
E – early (up to 65 days)
M – midseason (66-79 days)
L – late (80+ days)

DISEASE RESISTANCE:

A – alternaria (early) blight
As – alternaria stem canker
F – fusarium wilt, race 1
F2 – fusarium wilt, race 2
Ls – gray leafspot
N – nematodes
T – tobacco mosaic virus
V – verticillium wilt

'Ponderosa': I; OP; beefsteak; L; pink; heirloom
Also called 'Pink Ponderosa'; mild 12-oz. fruits with few seeds;
susceptible to cracking and sunscald (yellow and red forms available)

'Porter': I; OP; cherry; M; pink-red; heirloom
Egg-shaped, meaty 1-oz. fruits; Texas variety that thrives in heat and drought

'Principe Borghese': I; OP; drying; M; red; Italian heirloom
1-oz. plum-shaped fruits for sun-drying

'Pruden's Purple': I; OP; standard; M; pink-purple; heirloom
Flattened, meaty 1-lb. fruits; potato-leaf foliage

'Quick Pick': (VFF2NTA); I; H; standard; E/M; red
Meaty 5-oz. fruits; heavy yields; excellent disease resistance

'Red Currant': I; OP; dwarf; M; red
Different species *(Lycopersicon pimpinellifolium);* tiny, currant-sized fruits
('Yellow Currant' also available); large yields; often container-grown as
ornamental

'Roma VF': VigD; OP; paste; M/L; red
Fleshy, plum-shaped 2-oz. fruits for paste and sauce; rich flavor
(disease-resistant form of 'Roma')

'San Marzano'

'Rutgers': (F); VigD; OP; standard; L; red
  8-oz. fruits with mild flavor; high yields; widely adapted old favorite
  (hybrid forms with more disease resistance also available)

'San Marzano': I; OP; paste; L; red; Italian heirloom
  Also known as 'Italian Canner'; mild-flavored 3-inch-long fruits set in
  clusters; good for drying

'Sausage': I; OP; paste; M; red; heirloom
  Also listed as 'Red Sausage'; large, 6-inch-long banana-shaped fruits;
  paste and sauce variety

'Siberia': D; OP; standard; E; red; Russian variety
  Sets fruit at extremely low temperatures; 3-oz. fruits with fair flavor;
  good high-altitude variety

'Solar Set': (VFF1A); D; H; standard; M; red
  High-yielding plants bred to set fruit at high temperature; uniform 8-oz. fruits

'Striped German': I; OP; beefsteak; L; bi-color
  Mennonite heirloom (also listed as 'Old German'); yellow and red 1-lb. fruits
  with excellent flavor; likes heat but does not tolerate drought

'Stupice': I; OP; standard; E; red
  Short-season variety from Czechoslovakia; large crop of 2-oz. fruits;
  compact vines with potato-leaf foliage

'Taxi'

I – indeterminate
D – determinate
Vig – vigorous
OP – open pollinate
H – hybrid
E – early (up to 65 days)
M – midseason (66-79 days)
L – late (80+ days)

DISEASE RESISTANCE:

A – alternaria (early) blight
As – alternaria stem canker
F – fusarium wilt, race 1
F2 – fusarium wilt, race 2
Ls – gray leafspot
N – nematodes
T – tobacco mosaic virus
V – verticillium wilt

'Sub-Arctic Maxi': D; OP; standard E; red
Bred for extremely cold climates; 2½-oz. fruits; best of the Canadian Sub-Arctic series

'Sungold': (FT); I; H, cherry; E; gold
Long trusses of superbly flavored, crack-resistant 1-inch fruits; heavy yields; Japanese variety

'Supersteak': (VFN); I; H; beefsteak; M/L; red
1-lb. fruits with rich, tangy flavor; won't set fruit in extreme heat or cold; plants require support; susceptible to cracking

'Sweet 100': I; H; cherry; E; red
Best of the red cherry varieties; huge crop of 1-inch fruits in grape-like clusters; should be staked and pruned ('Sweet Million' is a disease-resistant form of 'Sweet 100')

'Sweet Chelsea': (VFF2NT); I; H; cherry; E; red
Low-acid, sweet 1½-inch fruits; drought-tolerant

'Taxi': D; OP; standard; E/M; yellow
Firm 5-oz. fruits; compact vine requires no staking; widely adapted

'White Beauty'   'Yellow Pear'

'Tiny Tim': (As); D; OP; cherry; E; red
Dwarf variety (13-inch vine, ¾-inch fruits) with rugose foliage;
often grown as ornamental; does best in pots or hanging baskets

'Toy Boy': (VF); D; H; cherry; E; red
Dwarf variety for container culture; 1-inch fruits

'Tropic': (VFAsNALsT); O; OP; standard; M/L; red
Thick-walled 8-oz. fruits; exceptional disease resistance; bred for hot,
humid regions; popular greenhouse variety

'Tumbler': D; H; cherry; E; red
Sweet 1-inch fruits; bred for hanging baskets and pots

'Valley Girl': D; H; standard; E/M; red
Sets fruit in heat or cold; firm, crack-resistant 7-oz. fruits

'Whippersnapper': D; OP; cherry; E; pink-red
Dwarf trailing variety for hanging baskets and pots;
¾-inch oval fruits; do not prune

'White Beauty': I; OP; standard; L ; white; heirloom
Also listed as 'Snowball'; ivory-white, fleshy 8-oz. fruits; sweet flavor

'Whopper': (VFNT); I; H; standard; M; red
Favorite Southern variety but widely adapted; 12-oz. fruits; heavy yields

'Yellow Bell': I; OP; paste; E; yellow; heirloom
Tennessee variety; clusters of sweet, rich 3-inch-long fruits;
adapted to cool conditions

'Yellow Pear': (FAs); I; OP; cherry; M; yellow; heirloom
Waxy, 2-inch-long pear-shaped fruits; heat-resistant; widely adapted
('Red Pear' is also available)

DELAYED GRATIFICATION:
Using the Harvest

Tomato Soup

Wash, scrape and cut small the red part of three large carrots, three heads of celery, four large onions and two large turnips, put them into a saucepan, with a tablespoonful of butter, and half a pound of lean new ham; let them stew very gently for an hour, then add three quarts of brown gravy soup, and some whole black pepper, with eight or ten ripe tomatas; let it boil an hour and a half, and pulp it through a sieve; serve it with fried bread cut in dice.

N.K.M. Lee, *The Cook's Own Book,* 1832

TOMATO RECIPES have changed as much as tomato varieties over time: finding a seed catalogue today that sells 'Fiji Island', a 19th-century egg-sized yellow tomato, is as unlikely as finding a cook whose tomato soup contains three quarts of brown gravy soup. While the loss of tomato varieties is cause for regret, the changes in tomato cuisine have been nothing but good, as the following recipes prove. For more ways to use your crop, see "Additional Resources," page 101.

TOMATO MATH

You only need to compare the price of tomatoes in the supermarket—anywhere from 99¢ to $2.99 a pound—with the cost of home-grown fruits to know that growing your own is good business: one 25¢ tomato seedling should yield about 10 pounds of fruit, for a price tag of 2½¢ per pound.

TOMATO SALSA

You can reduce the fire in this basic salsa recipe from *Harrowsmith Country Life* magazine—called by one taster "hot enough to make a gringo weep"—by seeding the chilies.

1½ lbs. ripe tomatoes, cored and
    halved (about 4)
1 tbsp. vegetable oil
1 small onion, chopped (¼ cup)
3 jalapeño or serrano chilies, chopped
    (2-3 tbsp.)
Salt to taste

Preheat broiler. Lightly grease or apply nonfat cooking spray to a baking sheet and place tomatoes on it, cut-side down. Brush with 1 tsp. of the oil. Broil until the skins split and blacken, about 10 minutes. Let cool, remove any very black pieces of skin and coarsely chop.

Place tomatoes, onions and chilies in a food processor or blender and process until the mixture is well combined but retains some texture.

In a heavy skillet, heat the remaining oil over medium-high heat until almost smoking. Add tomato mixture and cook, stirring constantly until thickened, about 8 minutes. Season to taste.

Yield: about 2 cups.

PESTO WITH SUN-DRIED TOMATOES

The intense flavor of sun-dried tomatoes gives this simple-to-make pesto a special zip. It is dynamite on pizza, grilled fish or chicken.

1½ cups fresh basil leaves
3 tbsp. chopped sun-dried tomatoes,
    marinated in oil
3 cloves garlic
¼ cup freshly grated parmesan cheese
⅓ cup pine nuts
½ cup olive oil
Salt and freshly ground black pepper
    to taste

Combine basil, tomatoes, garlic, cheese and pine nuts in a food processor or blender. With the machine running, add the olive oil and blend. Season to taste.

Yield: about 1 cup.

Bruschetta is simple to prepare and makes a delicious appetizer.

BRUSCHETTA

Bruschetta is a traditional Italian antipasto made with bread, garlic and the year's first pressing of olive oil. This version enhances the traditional recipe with tomatoes, onions and watercress. Be sure to use good-quality bread and olive oil. If you prefer, you can prepare bruschetta outdoors on the grill rather than in the oven.

3 large tomatoes (1½ lbs.), cored, seeded and finely diced
¼ cup chopped watercress
2 tbsp. finely chopped green onions
4½ tbsp. olive oil
1 tbsp. red-wine vinegar
⅛ tsp. salt
½ tsp. freshly ground black pepper
1 8-oz. loaf French or Italian bread
1-2 cloves garlic, cut in half
2 tbsp. freshly grated parmesan cheese (optional)

In a small bowl, combine tomatoes, watercress, green onions, 1/2 tbsp. oil, vinegar, salt and pepper. Mix well and set aside.

Preheat broiler. In a small pan, warm the remaining 4 tbsp. olive oil over low heat. Slice bread into ¾–inch-thick slices. Place on a baking sheet and broil for about 1 minute on each side, or until golden brown. Rub each slice with garlic and place on a serving platter. Brush with warm oil and top each slice with the reserved tomato mixture. Sprinkle with cheese. Serve immediately.

Yield: about 20 pieces.

Tomato-onion soup, one of the hundreds of variations on the basic recipe.

TOMATO SOUP

There are hundreds of tomato soup recipes. This one comes from contributor Jane Good, whose friends already know that she is as skillful in the kitchen as in the garden. A basic recipe, it can be adapted to include your favorite herbs.

2 tbsp. olive oil
1 onion, finely chopped
2 cloves garlic, minced
½ cup finely chopped celery
½ cup finely chopped carrot
6 tbsp. fresh basil, finely chopped
2 cups tomato juice
2 cups chopped tomatoes
2 tbsp. finely chopped fresh parsley
Salt and freshly ground black pepper
   to taste

In a large, heavy pan, sauté onions in oil over medium heat until transparent. Stir in garlic, celery, carrot and basil. Add tomato juice, 2 cups water and chopped tomatoes. Bring to a boil. Reduce heat and simmer until vegetables are tender, about 15 minutes. Season to taste. Serve garnished with parsley.

Serves 6-8.

TABBOULEH

There are scores of recipes for tabbouleh, a Middle Eastern salad. This one takes advantage of a generous addition of garden-ripe tomatoes and can be made several days ahead and refrigerated.

1 ½ cup bulgar wheat

4 large tomatoes, cored, skinned
and finely chopped

2 cucumbers, peeled, seeded and
finely diced

¼ cup chopped parsley

¼ cup chopped green onion

¼ cup chopped fresh mint

⅓ cup olive oil

⅓ cup fresh lemon juice

Salt and black pepper to taste

Rinse bulgar in cold water and drain. In a small bowl, combine bulgar with 1 cup cold water and let stand 1 hour. Drain. In a medium bowl, combine bulgar, tomatoes, cucumbers, parsley, green onion, oil and lemon juice. Toss gently. Season.

Cover and refrigerate until serving, at least 2 hours.

Yield: 8 servings.

Garden-fresh canned tomatoes are well worth the effort come winter.

TOMATO SAUCE

Nothing could be easier—or taste better—than pasta topped with a simple tomato-basil sauce. Be sure the pasta is *al dente,* not overcooked.

3 tbsp. olive oil

1 small onion, coarsely chopped

6 cloves garlic, peeled and thinly sliced

6 large tomatoes (2½ lbs.), cored,
peeled and coarsely chopped

Salt and freshly ground black pepper
to taste

⅓ cup fresh basil leaves, chopped

1 lb. spaghetti

⅓ cup freshly grated Parmesan cheese

In a large skillet, heat oil over medium heat. Add onion and garlic and cook, stirring, until tender, about 3 minutes. Add tomatoes and simmer until thickened, about 20 minutes. Add basil. Season to taste.

In a large pot of boiling water, cook spaghetti until *al dente,* about 6 minutes. Drain and transfer to a warmed serving bowl. Add sauce and toss. Serve immediately, sprinkling with cheese.

Serves 4.

NUTRITION NUMBERS

Tomatoes are Americans' number-one source of nutrients from vegetables and fruits—but only because we eat more tomatoes each year (per person, an average of 18 pounds fresh and another 70 pounds in processed forms) than any other vegetable or fruit except the potato. When it comes to nutrition, however, the tomato ranks sixteenth among common fruits and vegetables, trailing broccoli, spinach, Brussels sprouts, lima beans, cauliflower, sweet potatoes and others.

Truth be told, tomatoes are mostly water and perhaps most laudable for what they don't contain in large—or any—amounts: fat, sodium and cholesterol. And there's more good news. Tomatoes are an excellent source of vitamin A (in the form of beta carotene), vitamin C and potassium. Plus new research has established that tomatoes are rich in lycopene, an antioxidant and cancer fighter credited with lowering the incidence of prostate cancer.

And there is a bonus for the backyard gardener: vine-ripened tomatoes contain more than twice as much vitamin C and beta carotene as supermarket tomatoes, which are picked "mature green" and ripened artificially with ethylene gas.

TOMATO & BREAD SALAD

Known as panzanella in Italy, this salad is a delicious way to use yesterday's bread. Anchovies, which cooks in Tuscany include, have been omitted from this recipe—you may wish to add them.

1-2 cups high-quality Italian bread, cubed
2 large tomatoes, cubed (1½ cups)
1 cucumber, peeled, seeded and diced
½ cup chopped red onion
6 leaves fresh basil, chopped
4 tbsp. olive oil
1¼ tbsp. red-wine vinegar
Freshly ground black pepper

Preheat the oven to 425° F. Spread the bread cubes in a single layer on a baking sheet and toast until golden and crisp, about 15 minutes. Set aside to cool. In a medium bowl, combine tomato, cucumber, onion, basil, vinegar and oil. Add croutons and toss. Sprinkle with black pepper.

Serves 4.

GAZPACHO

Nothing could be more cooling on a hot summer night than a bowl of gazpacho, which is really a salad in a soup dish. Easy to make, it can be prepared

Use your imagination in experimenting with your own variations on gazpacho. In the recipe for the soup above, yellow tomatoes were substituted for red.

ahead of time, refrigerated and brought out when it's time to eat.

2 cups reduced fat and low sodium
   chicken broth
2 cups tomato juice
2 tbsp. fresh lemon juice
2 tbsp. olive oil
1 tsp. sugar
5 large tomatoes, cored, peeled,
   seeded and chopped
1 cucumber, peeled and diced
1 bell pepper, seeded and diced
⅛ cup finely chopped green onion
3 cloves garlic, minced
1 tbsp. finely chopped fresh parsley
Hot pepper sauce to taste
Freshly ground black pepper to taste

In a large bowl, combine all ingredients. Season with hot pepper sauce and black pepper. Chill for at least two hours before serving.

Yield: 4-6 servings.

JUDY'S CHICKEN À LA CHASSEUR

A classic chausseur sauce is enriched with demi-glace and butter. This delicious chicken version includes traditional ingredients—mushrooms, shallots, broth, herbs and wine or brandy—and is also heart-healthy.

2½ lb. chicken, cut in pieces

¼ cup flour

½ tsp. salt

¼ tsp. freshly ground black pepper

¼ tsp. tarragon

3 tbsp. olive oil

4 shallots or green onions, chopped

¼ lb. fresh mushrooms, chopped

2-3 large tomatoes, cored, peeled
    and coarsely chopped

¾ cup reduced-fat low-sodium
    chicken broth

¼ cup brandy

3 tbsp. minced parsley

1½ tbsp. fresh lemon juice

Salt and freshly ground pepper to taste

In a paper bag, combine flour, salt, black pepper and tarragon. Dredge chicken. In a large, heavy skillet, sauté chicken pieces in olive oil over medium heat until golden brown on all sides. Add shallots or green onions, mushrooms, tomatoes, broth, brandy, 2 tbsp. parsley and lemon juice. Cover and simmer over low heat for about 45 minutes, or until chicken is tender. Before serving, season to taste and sprinkle with remaining parsley.

Serves 4-6.

FRIED GREEN TOMATOES

Fannie Flagg's *Fried Green Tomatoes at the Whistle Stop Cafe* (and the movie it inspired) only publicized what rural Americans have known for years: cook it right, and a green tomato is every bit as delicious as a ripe one.

4 large underripe green tomatoes,
    cored and cut into thick slices

2 large eggs

2 tbsp. milk

1 cup cornmeal

1 tsp. salt

¼ tsp. freshly ground black pepper

5 tbsp. vegetable oil

In a medium bowl, lightly beat eggs

EASY OFF

Removing the skin from a tomato is easy: immerse the fruits—one tomato at a time—in a pan of boiling water until the skin cracks, about 15 seconds. Remove immediately from the water, rinse in cold water, and set aside until cool enough to handle. The skin should slip off easily.

and milk. In a second bowl, combine cornmeal, salt and pepper.

In a heavy skillet, heat oil over medium heat. Dip tomato slices into egg mixture, then into cornmeal mixture. Place in single layer in skillet and cook until golden on one side. Turn and cook until golden on the other side, and the tomato is fork tender. Repeat with remaining slices. Drain on paper towels. Serve immediately.

Yield: about 15 slices.

OVEN-DRIED TOMATOES

You don't have to live in the Southwest—or own a dehydrator—to dry tomatoes. Plum tomatoes work best, but any type of tomato can be used. It takes 15 to 17 pounds of fresh tomatoes (about a half-bushel) to make one pound of dried tomatoes.

Preheat the oven to 165° F. Lightly grease or apply nonfat cooking spray to a baking sheet. Wash and dry the tomatoes. Remove cores and cut tomatoes in half, lengthwise, or in ⅜-inch slices. Place tomatoes on baking sheet in a single layer. (If using cherry tomatoes, halve and place on the baking sheet cut-side-up.)

Dry tomatoes in the oven, uncovered, until dry to the touch but still pliable—not brittle—about 8 hours. (Check oven hourly to avoid burning.)

Store dried tomatoes in airtight containers. (To use: rehydrate tomatoes for 3-10 minutes in boiling water and drain.) Or cover dried tomatoes with a good-quality olive oil and store in an airtight container for up to 6 months in the refrigerator.

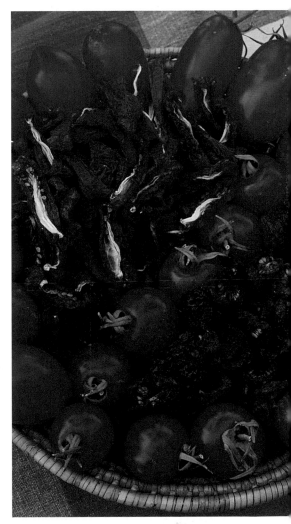

The intense flavor of sun- or oven-dried tomatoes is a delicious addition to pesto. Plum tomatoes are best for drying.

CANNED TOMATOES

Canning tomatoes in a water bath is easy and safe as long as you don't cut corners. These instructions are adapted from the *Ball Corporation's Blue Book: A Guide to Home Canning and Freezing* (1990). One bushel of tomatoes yields about 20 quarts.

Examine quart jars (use only jars manufactured specifically for canning) and sealing surfaces for nicks and cracks. Wash jars in hot, soapy water and rinse. Leave jars in clean, hot water. Place screw bands in a small pan filled with water and bring to a boil. Remove pan from heat and reserve until needed. Place canning lids in a small pan filled with water and place on the stove to simmer (180° F). Remove pan from heat and leave lids in hot water until needed.

Choose only blemish-free fruits, wash and drain. Remove skins (see "Easy Off," page 96) and core. Place tomatoes, whole or halved, in a large heavy kettle and add barely enough water to cover. Boil gently for 5 minutes.

Remove one jar from hot water and drain. Add 2 tbsp. lemon juice to each quart. Pack hot tomatoes into the jar, leaving ½-inch head space. Pour hot cooking liquid over tomatoes, leaving ½-inch head space. Run a nonmetallic spatula between toma-

Use freshly picked tomatoes with an assortment of vegetables, herbs and cheeses to top pizza.

toes to release any trapped air bubbles. Wipe the top and threads of jar clean with a damp cloth. Remove lid from simmering water with tongs and place on the jar. Screw band down evenly and firmly.

Stand each jar in a canner or large kettle of hot, not boiling, water. Water should cover jars by 1 to 2 inches. Cover the canner and bring water to a boil. Process quarts for 45 minutes at a gentle but steady boil. Remove jars from canner and set on a cloth surface. Do not retighten bands. Allow to cool, about 12 hours. Wash outside jar surface, remove bands and test seal. The center of the lid should be pulled down, creating a slightly concave sur-

YIELDS

1 large (10 oz.) tomato, peeled, seeded and chopped = ⅔ cup
1 large tomato, coarsely chopped with skin, seeds and juice = 1 cup
1 pound tomatoes = 2 large, 3 medium, 4 small or 20 cherry tomatoes

face. If you are unsure if the jar is sealed, gently push down the center. If it pushed down but then springs up, the jar is not sealed and should be refrigerated and eaten promptly. If the lid does not push down, the jar is sealed. Store in a dry, dark, cool place. (For pints, add 1 tbsp. lemon juice and process for 40 minutes.)

Top sliced tomatoes with a peppercorn vinaigrette or a splash of olive oil and a few fresh basil leaves.

ADDITIONAL RESOURCES

SEED & PLANT SOURCES

**Abundant Life Seed
Foundation**
P.O. Box 772
Port Townsend, WA
98368
(360) 385-5660
(seeds—OP varieties
only; many heirlooms;
most seeds certified
organic; non-profit
organization)
catalog, $2 donation

The Cook's Garden
P.O. Box 535
Londonderry, VT 05148
(802) 824-3400
(seeds—OP and hybrid
varieties, including many
European imports)
free catalog

**Early's Farm and
Garden Centre**
2615 Lorne Avenue
Saskatoon, SK S7J 0S5
Canada
(306) 931-1982
(seeds—hybrids and
OPs, including varieties
for cold, short-season
regions)
catalog, $2 in U.S.

Fedco Seeds
P.O. Box 520
Waterville, ME 04903
(207) 873-7333
(seeds—large collection
of hybrids and OPs,
including many
heirlooms; seed
cooperative)
catalog $2

Harris Seeds
P.O. Box 22960
Rochester, NY 14692-
2960
(716) 442-0410
(seeds—wide selection,
including many
proprietary hybrids with
improved disease
resistance)
free catalog

Heirloom Seeds
P.O. Box 245
West Elizabeth, PA
15088-0245
(412) 384-7816
(seeds—OP heirloom
varieties only)
catalog $1

J.W. Jung Seed Co.
335 South High St.
Randolph, WI 53957

(414) 326-3121
(seeds—OP and hybrid
varieties, many selected
for northern gardeners)
free catalog

**Johnny's Selected
Seeds**
310 Foss Hill Road
Albion, ME 04910-9731
(207) 437-9294
(seeds—large selection
of OPs and hybrids for
northern regions;
greenhouse varieties)
free catalog

Liberty Seed Company
P.O. Box 806
New Philadelphia, OH
44663-0806
(330) 364-1611
(seeds—good collection
of hybrid and OP
varieties chosen for the
Midwest)
free catalog

**The Natural
Gardening Company**
217 San Anselmo
Avenue
San Anselmo, CA 94960
(415) 456-5060
(plants—selection of

101

heirloom and other choice varieties; organically grown) free catalog

Park Seed Co.
P.O. Box 31
Greenwood, SC 29647-0001
(864) 223-7333
(seeds—mainly hybrid varieties, including many bred for the South)
free catalog

Peters Seed & Research
407 Maranatha Lane
Myrtle Creek, OR 97457
(541) 863-3693
(seeds—large collection of unusual OP varieties)
catalog $1

Pinetree Garden Seeds
P.O. Box 300
New Gloucester, ME 04260
(207) 926-3400
(seeds—good selection of hybrid and OP varieties for the home gardener)
free catalog

R.H. Shumway's
P.O. Box 1
Graniteville, SC 29829
(803) 663-3084
(seeds—OP and hybrid varieties, including many older home-garden favorites)
free catalog

Seed Savers Exchange
3076 North Winn Road
Decorah, IA 52101
(319) 382-5990
(seeds—membership gives access to largest collection of OP varieties available to gardeners; nonprofit organization)
membership, $25

Seeds Blüm
HC 33 Idaho City Stage
Boise, ID 83706
(800) 528-3658
(seeds—fine selection of OP and heirloom tomatoes, all chosen for flavor)
catalog $3

Seeds of Change
P.O. Box 15700
Santa Fe, NM 87506-5700
(505) 438-8080
(seeds—good collection

of OP and heirloom tomatoes, especially for the Southwest; organically grown seed)
free catalog

Seeds Trust-High Altitude Gardens
P.O. Box 1048
Hailey, ID 83333
(208) 788-4363
(seeds—tomatoes for short, cold seasons, including many Russian imports)
free catalog

Shepherd's Garden Seeds
6116 Highway 9
Felton, CA 95018
(408) 335-6910
(seeds—international collection of OP and hybrid tomatoes chosen especially for flavor)
free catalog

Southern Exposure Seed Exchange
P.O. Box 170
Earlysville, VA 22936
(804) 973-4703
(seeds—heirloom and OP varieties, many adapted for southern gardens)
catalog $2

Stokes Seeds Inc.
Box 548
Buffalo, NY 14240-0548
(716) 695-6980
(seeds—large, superb
collection of hybrids and
OPs for home and
market gardeners)
free catalog

**Territorial Seed
Company**
P.O. Box 157
Cottage Grove, OR
97424
(541) 942-9547
(seeds—wide selection
of OP and hybrid
tomatoes, including
many chosen for short
seasons)
free catalog

**Tomato Growers
Supply Co.**
P.O. Box 2237
Fort Myers, FL 33902
(941) 768-1119
(seeds—285 varieties of
tomatoes: hybrid and
OP, old and new)
free catalog

Totally Tomatoes
P.O. Box 1626
Augusta, GA 30903
(803) 663-0016
(seeds—more than 200
varieties for all needs
and regions)
free catalog

Twilley Seed Co., Inc.
P.O. Box 65
Trevose, PA 19053-0065
(800) 622-7333

(seeds—large collection
of hybrid tomatoes,
including many market
varieties)
free catalog

Vesey's Seeds Ltd.
P.O. Box 9000
Calais, ME 04619-6102
(902) 368-7333
(seeds—varieties for
short, cool seasons)
free catalog

W. Atlee Burpee & Co.
300 Park Avenue
Warminster, PA 18974
(800) 888-1447
(seeds—good selection
of varieties, including
many Burpee
introductions)
free catalog

103

FURTHER READING

DuBose, Fred. *The Total Tomato* (Harper & Row, 1985)

Doty, Walter, and A. Cort Sinnes. *All About Tomatoes* (Ortho Books, 1981)

Hoffman, Mable, *The Complete Tomato Cookbook* (HP Books, 1994)

Jordan, Michele Anna. *The Good Cook's Book of Tomatoes* (Addison-Wesley, 1995)

Luebbermann, Mimi. *Terrific Tomatoes* (Chronicle Books, 1994)

Nimtz, Sharon and Ruth Cousineau. *Tomato Imperative!* (Little, Brown and Company, 1994)

Shepherd, Steven. *In Praise of Tomatoes: A Year In the Life of A Home Tomato Grower* (HarperCollins, 1996).

Smith, Andrew. *The Tomato in America: Early History, Culture, and Cookery* (University of South Carolina Press, 1994)

NEWSLETTERS

Off the Vine
21-2 Latham Village Lane
Latham, NY 12110
$7 (3 issues per year)

The Tomato Club
114 East Main Street
Bogota, NJ 07603
$15.95 (bimonthly)

TOMATOES ONLINE

Web sites appear and disappear at lightning speed, but many Extension Service offices and state universities provide up-to-date information about growing tomatoes and other crops. One of the best, which also has a large list of links to other sites, is maintained at North Carolina State University: http://www4.ncsu.edu/eos/users/k/kemuelle/public/hp.html.

Another approach is to use a search engine, such as AltaVista. Be sure to narrow your request as much as possible: entering "tomato" alone will generate tens of thousands of listings. Computer-literate gardeners may also wish to participate in a Usenet newsgroup, such as rec.gardens, or sign up with one of several Listserv groups that specialize in gardening.

CONTRIBUTORS

This book was a collaborative effort. In addition to the contributing authors and 20 expert gardeners, my thanks go to James McFerson, USDA ARS Plant Genetic Resources Unit, Cornell University, Geneva, New York; Bill McDorman, Seeds Trust/High Altitude Gardens, Hailey, Idaho; Lorilyn Boone, Big Dipper Gardens, Fairbanks, Alaska; Tim Peters, Peters Seed & Research, Myrtle Creek, Oregon; and Marc Tosiano, National Agricultural Statistics Service, USDA, Concord, New Hampshire; Roger Shetelat, Tomato Genetic Resource Center, University of California, Davis, California; and Paul Thomas (ret.), Petoseed Co. Inc., Woodland, California.—K.D.C.

Garden designer and edible-landscape pioneer **Rosalind Creasy** lives in Los Altos, California. A popular horticultural lecturer, she is the author of *The Complete Book of Edible Landscaping* and *Cooking From the Garden,* both published by Sierra Club Books.

Karan Davis Cutler, who was guest editor of the award-winning *Salad Gardens* handbook (Brooklyn Botanic Garden, 1995), is a garden writer and magazine editor. She lives in northern Vermont, where summers are short and blackflies abundant.

Paul Dunphy grows all his own tomatoes—with plenty left over for the neighbors—in his western Massachusetts garden. A professional woodworker, freelance writer and editor, his garden articles have appeared in *Harrowsmith Country Life, Horticulture* and other magazines.

Horticulturist **Barbara Ellis** tends tomatoes and pets on her eastern Pennsylvania farm. A freelance writer, she is the co-editor of Rodale's *All-New Encyclopedia of Organic Gardening* (1992) and *The Organic Gardener's Handbook of Natural Insect and Disease Control* (Rodale, 1992).

In order to savor the juicy sweetness of summer, freelance garden writer and editor **Jane Good** *(The Gardener's Color Guide,* 1993) and her husband have grown—and supported—hundreds of tomato plants in their eastern Ontario garden for the past 22 years.

Shepherd Ogden lives in southern Vermont and is the owner of The Cook's Garden, a seed company specializing in vegetables and flowers for the kitchen garden. He is also the author of several garden books, including *Step By Step Organic Vegetable Gardening* (HarperCollins, 1992).

Aurelia C. Scott lives in Arroyo Seco, New Mexico, 7,700 feet above sea level, where the growing season is only 100 days long. When not gardening, Scott works as executive director of the local Habitat for Humanity affiliate, volunteers as a Master Gardener and writes for garden publications.

In addition to writing a weekly garden column for the *Fairbanks Daily News-Miner,* **Linden Staciokas** is a Master Gardener and Master Food Preserver. After three years in Barrow—where there are eight frost-free days per year—Staciokas has returned to Fairbanks. Gratefully.

Pat Stone wrestles blight, escaped cows and carpets of chickweed in his backyard garden and still finds time to publish *GreenPrints: The Weeder's Digest* four times a year. For subscription information, write P.O. Box 1355, Fairview, NC 28730.

ILLUSTRATION CREDITS

DRAWINGS by Steve Buchanan

PHOTOS
COVER AND PAGES 1, 8, 26, 48 TOP, 54, 66, 71, 91, 92, 93, 95, 97, 98, 99 BY ROSALIND CREASY
PAGES 4, 15 TOP AND BOTTOM BY CHRISTINE M. DOUGLAS
PAGES 9, 20 LEFT AND RIGHT, 31, 46, 56, 68, 70, 73 TOP, 74 TOP AND BOTTOM, 78 TOP, 82, 83, 85, 86, 87, 88 RIGHT, 100 BY DAVID CAVAGNARO
PAGE 23 BY FAITH ECHTERMEYER
PAGES 24, 27, 29, 33, 50, 81, 88 LEFT AND 96 BY DEREK FELL
PAGES 44, 48 BOTTOM, 62, 67, 69, 72, 73 BOTTOM, 75, 76, 84 LEFT AND RIGHT BY judywhite
PAGES 18, 45, 61, 64, 78 BOTTOM BY JERRY PAVIA
PAGE 52 BY AURELIA SCOTT
PAGE 58 BY PAT STONE
PAGE 60 BY CARL DUNCAN

INDEX

111

Gardening Books
FOR THE
Next Century

Published four times a year,
these award-winning books explore the
frontiers of ecological gardening.
Your subscription to BBG's **21st-Century
Gardening Series** is free with
Brooklyn Botanic Garden membership.

TO BECOME A MEMBER

please call (718) 622-4433, ext. 265.
Or, photocopy this form,
complete and return to:
Membership Department, Brooklyn Botanic Garden,
1000 Washington Avenue, Brooklyn, NY 11225-1099

YOUR NAME . . . .

ADDRESS . . . .

CITY/STATE/ZIP . . . .

PHONE . . . .

I want to subscribe to the 21st-Century Gardening Series
(4 quarterly volumes) by becoming a member of the
Brooklyn Botanic Garden:

☐ **$35 · SUBSCRIBER**   ☐ **$125 · SIGNATURE**

☐ **$50 · FAMILY/DUAL**   ☐ **$300 · SPONSOR**

TOTAL $ . . . .

FORM OF PAYMENT:

☐ CHECK ENCLOSED   ☐ VISA   ☐ MASTERCARD

CREDIT CARD# . . . .

EXP . . . .

SIGNATURE . . . .